COBWEBS
on the
CHANDELIER

Dorothy Monroe

ISBN-10: 1470025310
EAN-13: 9781470025311
Library of Congress Control Number: 2012902230
CreateSpace, North Charleston, SC

Illustrations by Jonathan Ball
Ball Design and Illustration

For James

And those who followed:

Steve
Dave
Melody
Andy
Nate
Kei

. . . without whom there'd have been no stories.

CONTENTS

GETTING TO KNOW
ALL ABOUT YOU

Jay and I were married on April Fools' Day. Were we tempting fate? Erma Bombeck once compared those who explain to those who don't. It takes a certain aplomb to

adopt that sophisticated stance, never explaining. I can't do it—I'm an explainer. We chose the date because of the Easter holiday so that our twelve siblings and their families could attend. Jay says, "I've been telling her 'April Fools' ever since. She's not convinced."

As we departed on our honeymoon, the subject of pooling our cash came up. I reached into the pocket of my coat and pulled out three cents.

Jay's reaction: "I didn't marry you for your money, but somehow I figured you for a little more than that."

M r .   F i x - I t

When Jay and I met with our pastor for obligatory pre-marital counseling, the pastor took us aback when he said, "Do you like each other?"

He quickly added, "I don't mean *love*. I mean *like*."

We looked at each other and laughed, but that question remains fixed in my mind. The rest of the conversation has faded from memory.

Since then I've developed a whole list of questions any prospective bride should consider. For example: Can he fix things? If so—what's *not* to like?

Jay grew up on a farm where there was a term for the kind of repairs I am apt to undertake—the Sam Treadwaller approach. Sam was a neighboring farmer whose solution to any mechanical malfunction was to slap it back together with baling wire and twine. Such repairs were a delaying tactic; eventually there would be a complete collapse. Jay, on the other hand, studies any mechanical problem. He hefts the offending machine and subjects it to a microscopic examination. He thumps and twists parts. He coaxes and wheedles gears and wheels. His repairs outlast the machinery itself.

"Why don't you take a little more time?" he suggests when I'm verbally abusing a failing machine. "Examine it. Look it over. Try to ascertain how it's supposed to work."

My perception is clouded by a sense of betrayal. These drones are supposed to make life easier.

One day my printer jammed with multiple sheets of paper that attempted to feed through in misaligned bunches. A gentle pull on the paper went unrewarded. I turned the machine upside down, yanked and tugged the sheets free of the roller, and grappled and twisted torn pieces from the grip of an invisible jaw. Finally I picked the last remnant out with a pair of tweezers. When the mechanism was cleared, I refilled the machine with fresh paper—only to have the machine repeat its bungling behavior.

I sought Jay out in his workshop. "I need a tool."

"Sure." Jay looked pleased. All of his admonitions were beginning to take hold, and his teaching was paying off. "What are you looking for?"

"I need an ax—to fix a printer problem." I grinned maliciously.

Jay dropped what he was doing and slogged toward my office.

Our teenage children were required to buy and insure their own vehicles. They started buying cars before computers resided under every hood. Back then an enterprising home mechanic could ascertain the root of a problem without the car being hooked up to an electronic problem-solver. The critical diagnostic tool was a good ear.

Jay—whose first car had been an old Ford Model A—was called upon to lend his ear to the kids as they went through a succession of used cars. Today their cars would be called preowned (such an ostentatious term—as if it were simply a stage in the car's evolution toward becoming a real vehicle). "Used" is definitely a more fitting description for the cars parked at the end of our driveway over the years. I remember them, with their drab colors, rusty dents, and scratches, as tired, indistinctive heaps of metal. They consumed not only gas and oil, but also enormous amounts of time to coax them into performing their daily duties. Jay assisted the kids with countless oil changes, tires, brake pads, radiators—and once, even a whole new engine. He had one of those little scooters that roll under the cars so that he could work on them. The only thing our garage lacked was a grease pit.

Recently a neighbor commiserated with Jay. "Sure miss those days when you could crawl under the hood and work on your own car."

Jay responded with a noncommittal "Hmmm."

Now he's fixing printers.

On Being a Good Sport

The couple that plays together stays together. (Feuding is not a sport.)

Jay and I tried a number of leisurely activities. Golf was too expensive for newlyweds and, when we could afford it, too discouraging. The percussive woodpecker sound made by a golf ball on a narrow fairway is not a happy one, especially when the drunken ball careens from one tree-lined side to the other.

Taking a tennis class with a ten-year-old is a sure way to kill your interest in the game. I watched helplessly as my child raced up to the net and back, banging balls in my direction. I developed tennis elbow and the accompanying dire prediction that I might never play again. It was okay by me; tennis is a sweaty sport.

In the end, fishing gets my vote.

We fished on the banks of Lake of the Ozarks on our honeymoon. In my frenzy to pack, I'd forgotten a jacket, so I stood wrapped in a cashmere dress coat, throwing out my fishing line hour after hour—without a bite.

I was tossing my line a hundred feet from Jay when he shouted, "Come quick!" He swung his pole high in the air, dangling his catch at the end of his line. I propped my pole and raced down shore to get a closer look. I stopped at the sight of his prize: a decaying, stinking, milky-eyed fish. It was our only catch on the trip.

Many fishing trips followed. For several years, we fished the bay waters off the coast of Mississippi. I learned to thread live shrimp bait on my hook. (I still haven't mastered worms!) Our catches included stingrays, eels, flounder, crab, speckled trout, redfish, and once—a turtle. Fishing is good training for life. It requires focus on the goal and the ability to reel in the prize. Nature reliably provides plenty of obstacles: winds blow, waves toss you about, and the sun bakes you. Some days the distractions are so overwhelming that you forget the goal—like a no-see-ums attack.

I've seen movies where a cloud of bugs drives the hero to dive into the water to escape the harassing insects. Those insects must have been no-see-ums. These miserable little gnatlike insects are torturous. They get caught in your hair, fly up your nostrils or into your open mouth, and buzz in your eyes. They're bloodsuckers. They threaten to convert you into an indoor recluse, but eventually the lure of fishing entices you back to the water.

Early in our married life, Jay's principal job on fishing trips was preparing the poles, baiting hooks, and untangling lines. He spent little time with his own line. His reward was a family of fishing enthusiasts. We've traveled from the headwaters of the Mississippi to the Gulf of Mexico on our fishing jaunts—with typical fisherman's luck (the biggest one always gets away) and plenty of tales.

The memory of Jay in his waders being drawn into the bottomless bay water mud remains one of my nightmares. I was a frantic bystander on the shore, shouting and waving my arms. He freed himself by scrambling out of his rubber suit as it was sucked into the silt at the bottom. During winter low tides, the top of those boots stuck out of the mud like a shadowbox picture—a skull-and-crossbones reminder.

One warm spring afternoon, Jay, our son Jeff, and I took our small boat out to fish under a bridge in Mississippi bay waters. We soon caught a couple of flounders and some speckled trout. Jeff stood tall in the middle of the boat, throwing out his line. I sat at one end of the boat, perched on the narrow seat, threading shrimp onto my hook. I stood and cast my line. My reel sang its clear-pitched whine, followed by a clunk. A weighty shrimp? Jeff turned to stare at me and it took me a minute to register what had happened. I'd hooked his glasses—*that* was that little clunk!

We added weights to our lines and began dropping our lines and dragging our hooks across the bottom. The glasses had to be somewhere within the small radius of the boat. The three of us spent the rest of the afternoon fishing for Jeff's glasses. Disappointment followed excited cries as we hooked weeds and junk. Finally we abandoned the search, drove to the mall, and found an optician so that Jeff could read again.

Somewhere down there lives a fish with corrected vision.

If Wishes Were Horses (Jay's Version)

It is possible to live with a man for fifty years and still not know his secret longings. I've had clues along the way, but I've failed to perceive or acknowledge them. A little slip of conversation last week highlighted the weight of all those years of desire, like eyeing a huge chocolate slab through the window of a closed candy store. If I'd been a game show contestant required to guess what was at the top of my husband's wish list, I'd have flunked. I've been living with a complete stranger.

Jay mused, "I think I'm the only one of my brothers and sisters (one of eight) who has *never* owned a pickup." His voice was laced with sadness. "A pickup makes life so much easier. No tying down the trunk lid with a load of lumber sporting a red flag flying behind. Think how easy it would be to haul this compost in a pickup." He was referring to five cubic yards of Cedar Grove compost dumped on our drive by a highly paid deliveryman.

"You've been spared," was my first response. (Wrong response! I'd failed to acknowledge his pain.) I challenged him. "I don't think your oldest brother ever owned a pickup."

"He did." Jay proceeded to describe it to me—color, make, model, and where and when he'd owned it.

"But you've had lots of vans . . . more than anyone else in your family."

"It's not the same. You can't do with a van what you can do with a pickup truck."

I have no love for pickups. For several years, one of our neighbors owned an ancient pickup. Its original color had faded to a dappled gray, and it was flecked with orange rust. It smoked and chugged when he fired it up—then it roared. Jed Clampett would have felt perfectly at home in it.

Most days my neighbor parked that pickup in front of my carefully tended flower beds, so that any guest's first glimpse of our house did not include my pink and yellow alstroemerias, my Mrs. D. W. Maxwell Cornish heath, my purple salvia, and my white snow-in-summer blooming under the purple smoke tree. No—their view was of that dreadful pickup!

I entertained vivid dreams of helping that pickup meet its end, but I could never summon the nerve to assist in its demise. Finally the neighbor gave it to one of his children. I reminded Jay about this.

"I was always hoping he'd give it to me."

I stared at him. For five years, he'd listened to me rant about that rattletrap. I knew I should be grateful; my husband didn't covet his neighbor's wife—he coveted his pickup!

I was hurt. If he'd really wanted a pickup, surely he could have mustered a good argument for purchasing one. We've always shared the budgeting. I've never been a witch-wife who controls the purse strings. Yet I admitted to myself that I'd have been a pretty hard sell. Four kids and you want a pickup? We don't need three cars! A pickup is a greedy gas hog.

By evening I'd come up with a peace offering. "Sweetheart, I'll sprinkle some of your ashes in a pickup so you can spend eternity in the vehicle of your dreams."

Mr. Neatnik

During the hottest summer months, a family struggle reached a stalemate. The presence of the blue-flowered, plastic wading pool in the center of our drive made war impossible. When the wind shifted to the northwest and the nights cooled, hinting at the approaching fall, it was apparent that Jay was gearing up for a new offensive.

One evening I caught sight of him from the front window as he pulled his car into the driveway and stopped. A coaster wagon, Mark's trike, and Lissy's blue five-speed stood like guards expecting a skirmish. Jay flung the car door open and unwound himself from the front seat. His suit was wrinkled, and his tie was loosened at the neck. In a state of complete and deliberate calm, he pulled the strung-out line of vehicles to a spot on the grass and climbed back in his car. His face betrayed no anger; my husband is a patient man.

I glimpsed his unreadable face as he paused again at the garage door. What passed through his mind in that instant before he slid the door up to reveal the contents? Was it dread? Anticipation? Resignation? Did he view it as a matching of wits? The door opened to reveal the most recent clutter. He left his car outside.

At the dinner table, he served notice. "Saturday we are cleaning the garage."

The five of us nodded, and I murmured a note of sympathy. This eternal battle pitted the aggressor against lackadaisical foes. Jay was outnumbered.

According to Webster, a garage is a shelter for automobiles. Jay wanted to use it for its original purpose. He wanted to park his car inside it. Our garage, however, was like an ancient suitcase returning from a summer's travels, bursting at the seams. The kids and I tucked trifles into every space. Our instinct was to save, pile, and postpone discarding decisions. Some of our reticence to throw stuff away was due to the finality of the trash truck. When we faced decisions about what to do with cardboard boxes, empty plastic flower pots, flattened bicycle tires, rusting red wagons with two wheels missing, and other sundry items, we solved the problem by stashing them in a corner of the garage. Our garage was a halfway house for faded furniture.

Early Saturday morning, we all pitched in to help. We littered the front lawn.

Our thirteen-year-old remarked in a flash of brilliance, "Dad, did you ever think about it—the difference between garage and garbage is only a 'b'?"

From the look on Jay's face, I knew it was no revelation.

The boys wheeled out bicycles and the trike. Lissy lugged out the dogs' trays and dishes. We stacked garbage cans, an old metal milk box (an antique), tennis rackets, golf clubs, a box of balls, piles of assorted pieces of wood, garden stakes, and various bottles of differing sizes that were sure to come in handy. Jay placed an empty garbage can conspicuously on the drive. He proceeded to discard rolled-up weekly circulars, plastic wrap from newspapers, and sacks with stray pieces of dog food rolling around at the bottom.

"No," Jay answered a passerby, "it's not a garage sale—just wishful thinking on my part." My lanky, six-foot husband grinned.

When the garage was finally emptied of all its contents, the crew was dismissed. Jay surveyed the scene. His efforts to maintain space inspired his ingenuity. His first project was designing a shelf for the sports balls. He carefully measured round holes in a long board. There would be a hole for every ball.

By late afternoon, the garage floor was hosed and drying. Bicycles were hung on hooks, lawn chairs dangled from nails, and the footballs, basketballs, baseballs, and soccer balls were all lined up on the new shelf. Garden hoses wound around curving hangers. Even the dogs were quiet in their pens.

Dressed in his oldest work jeans and buckled overshoes, Jay wiped perspiration from his forehead. He stepped back on the drive to admire his newly organized garage. He basked in victory and summoned the crew. He presented the finished product with outstretched arms.

"There! Now if everyone will try, we can keep this place in order. I'll park my car inside all winter."

A kite floated gently to his feet from its appointed spot on the wall. For a brief instant, there was an inexplicable glint in his eye as Jay dangled his foot above the kite's wooden frame. A half-smile crept across his face. Then he stepped aside and, laughing sheepishly, bent over to pick it up.

"Danny'd miss his kite."

He propped up the kite and wound its string around the nail again. He shrugged his shoulders and sighed, accepting the advance and retreat of daily battle.

"Tonight the car goes in."

HOUSEKEEPING

Housekeeping is a blind alley occupation. A novice housekeeper doesn't realize how dangerous it is until the first day she picks up the toilet bowl cleaner and discovers that she could die if she mixes it with bleach. A further

admonition on the bottle is underlined: <u>Do Not Close Toilet Bowl Lid.</u> Would closing the lid convert the toilet bowl into a pressurized bomb, triggered to explode when the lid gets lifted?

Household disinfectants are harmful if breathed, fatal if swallowed. One faulty maneuver on a step stool carries the risk of broken bones. Small appliances can electrocute you.

I want hazard pay.

Cobwebs on the Chandelier

I'm familiar with the ritual called housecleaning. I participate, but when it comes to chandeliers, I draw the line. You know the scenario—an indomitable housekeeper stands up to a haughty matron and declares, "I don't do windows." I eyeball my reflection in the mirror and state, "I don't do chandeliers."

There is a good reason why the glint of the incandescent bulbs in my chandelier illuminates tiny wisps and trails of industrious spiders. It has nothing to do with my opinions on women's work. It's much more practical. The last time I tried to dust the chandelier, I nearly killed myself. It's not worth the risk.

I was preparing for one of my semi-annual dinner parties and, after spreading the table pad and topping it with a freshly laundered, lace-trimmed tablecloth, my eyes were drawn to one of those aforementioned webs. Nothing spotlights dirt and grime like the impending arrival of guests. I pushed the light switch and saw a maze of webs shining among the crystal prisms.

I rummaged through the rag drawer until I found an old flannel pajama shirt, torn at the elbows, ripped at the shoulder, and transformed into rag—the perfect dusting cloth. I tore off a sleeve and lay the rest of the shirt under the chandelier to catch any drifting specks of dust. I mounted the padded seat of a chair in my stocking feet and began dusting the chandelier.

It's hard to tell where you've started when you dust a chandelier. When it seemed as though I'd gone full circle in the winding, I swished over another little light and its accompanying glass and let the fixture swing back to unwind. All was well. Then I made my mistake. *Aha!* I thought, looking at the soiled rag, if the fixture was *that* dirty, the gold chain from which it hangs must be equally disgraceful.

Gingerly, I placed one foot in the middle of the table on the flannel pajama shirt and eased my weight on it. Zip! My foot went sliding on the sled of tablecloth and pad, and when I was full-split, I toppled backwards. The chair skidded out from under me, and my head skimmed the corner of the china closet and slammed on the floor. I lay motionless as the thud resounded in my head and body. Gradually I realized in my stunned state that I had to rescue myself. My doors were locked and my husband wasn't home. There wasn't even a dog to lick my face!

Slowly I gathered myself together and clutched the back of the chair, surveying the wreckage. I swore. The new gold candles—the ones I'd purchased on a special outing to the store—were broken. I'd cracked the leg of the chair. My shoulder ached. My toe was bleeding through a torn stocking. In short—it was a catastrophe.

That evening, Jay and I were stretched out watching the evening news when the announcer intoned: "Most accidents happen in the home."

An amused voice beside me chimed in. "And here we have the living proof."

I groaned. Should I remind him of another well-known fact? When it comes to violence, one has more to fear from a relative than a stranger.

Confessions of an Inept Mechanic

I had to be rescued from my own garage—along with three children who were late for school—trapped by a medieval iron bar. I'm a complete klutz when it comes to machines, and it has nothing to do with genetics. My mother rewired her own kitchen.

My father encouraged me to study home economics. "Such good preparation for a woman," he said.

Instead I became a social scientist, studying sociology and psychology for my bachelor's degree and post-graduate courses. As it turned out, we were both wrong—I should have become a mechanic.

I did make one attempt at self-improvement. I took a course titled "Household Equipment 101." My most vivid memory of the class is the professor grinding oatmeal into a carpet with a high-heeled shoe—the first step in choosing a new vacuum cleaner. By the time I purchased a vacuum cleaner, I had forgotten about the oatmeal.

When I acquired a house of my own, I discovered that knowing how to put a plug on an iron is dispensable knowledge. I've developed a whole new approach to machines—a kind of machine psychology. Each machine is unique in my eyes, endowed with its own capabilities, programmed to perform or fail. Supposedly machines come off an assembly line as exact replicas, but I'm convinced that built into them, somewhere, there is a difference. I do my best to understand my machines' quirks. I'm a meek custodian, trying to keep some semblance of control over a household of eccentric servants.

My coffee pot will only perk if it's plugged into the top outlet. My toaster is not as fickle; it works on either outlet. However, I can forget trying to toast two slices in succession, because it will spit the bread back in my face. It hates to be hurried. My garbage disposal is on a finicky diet; bones get stuck in its throat. It gums banana peels like a toothless old man, swirling them around, taking nary a nibble or bite.

Some machines are sensitive to criticism. My dishwasher started making strange sounds.

"That machine is going to quit on me. Maybe I need a new one," I worried aloud to Jay. He took out the motor and hauled it to a repair shop.

"Sorry, we need to work on the whole machine," he was told.

So Jay lugged the motor home and put it back in the dishwasher. We haven't heard a rumble since.

Other machines are impervious to threats. My first vacuum cleaner gobbled objects whole and then—realizing it had consumed too much too soon—regurgitated. It would spew its half-digested contents in a fine spray, filling the room with grit and grime. Long hairs caught on the gasket and flew like tiny flags in the wind. Repeated trips to the repair shop made no impression on the cantankerous machine, so I returned it to its maker.

Children often make liars of their parents. If you tell Aunt Helen that Johnny never eats tomatoes, at that moment, he'll give you an astonished look and proceed to wolf down three of them. Machines behave in much the same way. My neighbor asked to borrow my warming tray.

"Wish you could," I replied, "but it isn't heating." To prove my point, I plugged it in, and a warm glow spread over its surface. I could almost see the smirk on its face.

I have discovered that if an appliance is watched too carefully, it will stray at the first opportunity. One dishwasher in particular had been run under the closest supervision, with the utmost of caution. It never once displayed delinquent tendencies—until the mistress was away. The husband loaded it up, poured in the soap, turned the power on, and went to bed. In the morning, he tramped barefoot down the hall and encountered a stream of water flowing from the kitchen. He found the maniacal machine frantically pumping water onto the floor, hours after he innocently assumed it would shut itself off.

Rebellious machines are easily recognizable. They tend to strike when it hurts most. Our air conditioner quit on the hottest day of the year, in the first hours of a long weekend. It must have known that repairmen charge overtime on holidays and demand cash. Another air conditioner in our neighborhood broke down twice last summer—once on the Fourth of July and again on Labor Day. Don't tell me that wasn't deliberate.

Machines are like people in the sense that they balance out. For every uncooperative, obstinate machine, there's an equally cooperative, servile appliance. While one peters out without half-trying, another will work itself to death. When I find such a slave, I cherish it. My clothes dryer may have to be coaxed into starting with a twist or two of the drum and it may overheat after two loads, but it has worked predictably for fifteen years. My washing machine has churned out hundreds of loads of damp, clean clothes. I pamper it.

There are two questions I'm often asked by newer housewives: "How do you choose one?" and "Can you leave them unattended?"

In answer to the first question—when I replace a machine, I read all available literature and compare every feature of each machine. I interview friends and neighbors who own the same machine and shop carefully. When things go awry, I curse my luck.

As for the second question—I refuse to babysit machines. If they misbehave while I am away, I accept my fate.

Although, just to be safe, I leave the dishwasher door open; check the faucets; turn off the gas; unplug the toaster, TV, coffee pot, lamps, and blender; shut off the water hoses to the washing machine; flip the furnace button off; and tape the freezer door shut.

Oh, for an Empty Gas Tank

I know it sounds hard to believe with today's strained budgets, but there are times when a brimming gas tank is a curse!

Jay and I were sitting on the front steps, drinking coffee and enjoying a peaceful Saturday morning. The kids were playing catch in the park across the street.

"I wonder what that spot is under the van." Jay put down his coffee and went to investigate. He dropped to the concrete and slithered on his back under the van.

"Well?" I crouched by a wheel, trying to see what was going on.

"Oh, #$%^&!" Jay scrambled out from under the van and raced for the garage. He banged through drawers, grabbed something, and tore back to slide under the van again.

"What's the matter? What's happening?"

"Gas tank," was all I heard. I could smell that much.

In a few minutes, Jay inched his way out from under the van, more slowly this time. He sighed, defeated.

"I touched a damp spot on the gas tank and a piece of metal dropped out—about the size of a pencil lead." He got up slowly. "I stopped it for now with a dab of caulking, but we have to get it welded right away. The metal around it could go any time."

He headed for the house, pulling off his gassy shirt. I trailed him.

"When did you last fill up?"

"Yesterday," I faltered. "I put in twenty-two gallons."

We stared at each other. Then he heaved his shoulders and plodded on. My stomach sank.

Jay washed up and began calling garages. "Nothing open …" He finished dialing the last number. "We'll have to wait until Monday. I can drive it to work and try to find a repair shop. Meanwhile we'll roll it to the end of the drive."

Visions of horror flashed through my mind. Gasoline and a wind-driven spark—fire engines—body parts flying. I shut my eyes tight. The images replayed themselves over and over like a melody in my brain.

The caulking held the rest of the day and all day Sunday. On Monday morning, Jay drove the van in search of a repair shop. I tried to contain my imagination. I remembered reading that one gallon of gasoline has the explosive power of ten sticks of dynamite. Multiply that by twenty-two!

That evening, Jay returned with the van. He stopped at the end of the drive.

"Fixed?" I asked.

"Nope! The guy took one look at it and said, 'No way!' He can't work on a full tank and fire laws won't permit him to store twenty-two gallons of gasoline in his shop. 'Drive it out,' was his advice." Jay shrugged. "Guess I'll have to."

I thought of my husband—the father of my children, breadwinner, and love of my life. "No way! That's maniacal! It's not safe . . . driving on the interstate with a caulked gas tank. I won't let you."

"Well, *you* certainly can't drive it," he countered. Silence followed. Then Jay made his decision. "We'll siphon the gas."

Siphoning is not as simple as it seems. First there is the matter of positioning. After considerable maneuvering, Jay finally got our two vehicles parked for the procedure. His car was at a lower level, and the van—facing the opposite direction—was up on the curb. He found a piece of flexible hose in the garage.

I bantered as he worked. "I don't think it's safe. I've read about these things . . . people getting gas in their lungs."

Jay gave me a withering look. He worked, sucking the end, trying to get a flow.

"It's tricky," he informed me. "You've got to get the flow going and then put the hose in the other car."

A small trickle of gas gurgled forth. He whipped the end into the other gas tank. The flow stopped. Jay wiped the hose off and tried again.

"Be careful. That's gas!"

The flow stopped again. Jay's face was red.

"All right, all right. There's a kit you can buy. Take my car down to the shopping center."

I felt like a criminal asking for a siphoning apparatus; I was compelled to explain my predicament to every store clerk. Finally I found an inexpensive kit.

Jay viewed my purchase with little enthusiasm.

"Flimsy," he observed. He put the plastic tube in the gas tank and squeezed on the bulbous end. It snapped off. "Cheap kit!"

Jay muttered some choice words, got a knife, and tried to repair it. The hose and bulb were constructed as one unit—with escaping air, there was no suction. It was hopeless.

"The store is closed. We'll have to get another one tomorrow," I observed.

"Why don't you call some rental places? They might have a better kit," Jay suggested as we locked up for the night. We went to bed with our bomb parked at the end of the drive.

On Tuesday morning, I checked the van. It wasn't leaking yet. I renewed my telephone search for a siphoning kit, and I found a rental store fifteen miles away.

"Yup, lady, we got one. Open all day until six. Yes, ma'am."

All day I kept my eye on the cement under the van. I had a bad feeling.

"Mom . . . " Danny's nose wrinkled as he came in after school. "It smells like gas outside."

I tore for the window. A small stream spouted under the van. I raced for the garage and pawed through a drawer. Where was that caulking? I slammed the drawer. I took the steps two at a time for the boys' room. Clay—Silly Putty—Play Dough—bubble gum. I scrounged through the room and found a dirty green, pliable lump. I ran to the van, flopped onto my back, and scooted beneath, the rough concrete scratching my bare legs. I plunged my hand into the stream of gas and covered the hole. After working the lump in my other hand, I dried the surface around the hole with my shirtsleeve, and then carefully plastered the hole with the green glob. It stuck.

I slid out from under the van. How long would it take for gasoline to eat through green gluck? It was probably a good idea to chew some bubble gum. I went to take a shower.

The minute Jay pulled into the drive, I was out of the house. "Give me your keys. I have to hurry. The rental place closes at six." I drove the thirty miles to the rental shop.

When I returned with the kit, Jay took the long plastic hose and fed it into the van's gas tank. He squeezed the bulb and gave me a peculiar look.

"Didn't the guy check it out before he gave it to you?" I shook my head. "There's a hole in the #$%^& thing!"

I checked my watch and ran for the house. "Maybe if I call the rental store, the man will wait for me."

By seven o'clock, Jay had fed a fourth plastic hose into the gas tank, squeezed a bulb, and—miracle of miracles— a trickle of the golden liquid flowed from the van to the car. Minutes passed as three-quarters of a tank of gas transferred from one to the other.

The next morning, Jay took the van to the welder again. As the tank was nearly empty, the welder agreed to work on it. By Friday the gas tank was repaired.

I learned two things from this experience: A full gas tank can be a curse . . . and there's never a gas thief around when you need one.

Life Changers

I scanned the list of the top innovations of the last thirty years—*life changers,* according to judges at a leading business school. The Internet was prominent on the list, along with the cell phone and the marvels of medical imaging.

What struck me was how few innovations were geared toward housewives. The Internet is great, but it can't fix dinner or mop a floor. What are my candidates for life-changing inventions from my earliest days as a housewife (aka cleaning lady, laundress)? Here's my list:

Self-defrosting refrigerator-freezer

Defrosting and cleaning the refrigerator was a household job I postponed often. It was only when I could no longer jam food into the tiny space left in the freezer and ice became the dominant resident of the machine that I would tackle the job. The ice buildup on those old freezers was as stubborn as the polar icecaps before global warming.

The first task in cleaning out the frost-encrusted interior was to sort dishes of food, wrapping the ones to be salvaged in layers of newspaper and packing them in an ice chest. Tossing the remaining items that were past their prime was the second task. In those days we had no "best before" dates with their implied death sentences. We relied on our senses: Was the food covered with a little blanket of mold? Did it stink? Had it become a desiccated relic? (Why is it that we age our leftovers before we discard them?)

Once the interior was cleared, pans and baking sheets of hot water were placed—one on every shelf, several in the freezer space—to begin the melting process. I covered the floor in front of the refrigerator with large bath towels to soak up the inevitable pools of water from the melting ice and spills. Since I was impatient for the hot water to do its trick, I'd enlist the hair dryer to speed up the process. Finally, armed with an ice pick, I'd begin chopping and promise myself that next time I'd do this job before the layers of ice became cemented to the sides and shelves. (Invariably, the next time I'd have waited too long.)

The magic of the self-defrosting refrigerator-freezer has one drawback. Yesterday I was astonished to read on a package of frozen vegetables "Best used by 01-10-08". Do vegetables four years past their prime revert to compost? Had they become frozen fossils—shriveled, shrunken carcasses in their plastic wrap? I didn't bother to find out; I threw them in the yard waste can.

Self-cleaning ovens

Before I had a self-cleaning oven, I'd get apoplectic about a pie boiling out of its crust and depositing a scorched layer of caramel glaze on my oven bottom. It took a hatchet to penetrate and chip that mess off the bottom. Grease spatters were permanent decorations on my oven walls. By the time I'd get around to cleaning the oven, I'd risk asphyxiation or permanent lung scarring from inhaling the potent chemicals of oven cleaner. Those cleaners (the brand names suggested supermen) stank up the whole house. I was absolutely fascinated by my first self-cleaning oven—it could be transformed into an incinerator. Thanksgiving turkeys: bubble over to your heart's content!

Glass cooktops

What a delight to simply wipe off a glass stovetop! I have slit my fingers trying to disengage burner pans for scouring. Burnt crumbs always seemed to escape into the nether regions of the stove—beyond reach, but a glaring indictment to the eye. Sometimes they caught fire when I turned on a burner. Food bits on the coils were guaranteed to smoke and smell like toxic waste. No more frantic shopping trips for clean burner pans before the houseguests arrive!

Nonstick pans

There is debate about whether or not Teflon is a health hazard, but believe me—housewives of yesteryear died early from the strain of hacking at burned-on grease and food in the bottom of a tippy, pitted, black-bottomed pan. My sister and I fought over who had to wash (as opposed to dry) dishes. Those horrid black pans with their encrusted layers were the source of our fights.

Microwave ovens

I've gained weight since I got married—from eating my words. When microwave ovens were first introduced, I regarded them with disdain. Why would I need such a device, I wondered. I was an at-home mother; I could plan meals and allow for the time it took to cook food normally. I was lured into purchasing my first microwave by the promises of quick defrosting and reheated foods retaining their original flavor. What a revolution in cooking patterns! Now it's my stove that sits idle.

No-wax and preserved wood floors

As a new housewife, I was seduced into thinking that a clean floor had to shine. The ultimate reward was looking at the floor and seeing my reflection. This required a layer of wax, buffed to a high gloss. I quickly discovered that wax only wears in the center of a room. I couldn't seem to train my children to walk at the edges of a room and to scuff their toes under the counters, wearing away the wax evenly.

After waxing the floors several times without first applying wax remover, the rooms were outlined in ugly, yellow, wax buildup. Those ribbons screamed "lazy house-keeper"—wax buildup was a badge of shame. It was time to get out the wax remover and putty knife to scrape away the offensive gunk. How liberating it is to have floors with a permanent shine.

Wooden floors can now be embalmed so that they are impervious to wear and grime. The treatment is done by professionals and requires abandoning the house for a few days. Once, I opened a closet not properly aired after the treatment and was nearly overcome by the fumes—but it sure beats scrubbing and polishing.

Wash and wear fabric

I have vivid childhood memories of my grandmother spending hours at our house, standing over an ironing board with a bushel of wrinkled clothes at her feet. The mere preparation of clothes for ironing was a big project. They had to be starched, and the best starch was cooked.

Chalky, white, powdered starch was stirred into a big pot of cold water. Constant stirring was required to keep it from becoming lumpy while it cooked into a thick, pasty mass. Garments were doused in this cooled glob, wrung out, and hung on outdoor lines, where they were monitored for just the right degree of dampness. (If they got too dry, the wrinkles couldn't be ironed out.) Damp, starched items were rolled up and covered, removed one at a time, and pressed. At day's end, any leftover starched pieces were bagged for the next day and put into the freezer. Items not properly cared for would mildew, with clusters of gray mold weaving their tentacles into the fabric, never to be clean again.

The ironing board was a treadmill for the housewife. I've discarded mine. An iron makes a good bookend and, if you're into book burning, just plug in the iron.

Garment tags with printed care instructions

Today's housewives cannot imagine the trials of earlier years when sorting clothes for laundering or dry-cleaning was like pulling the handles of a slot machine. You never knew what that pull would bring.

The first puzzle was identification of the fabric. Was it cotton, rayon, silk, wool, nylon, or a blend of any and all of them? If it was a blend, which element was primary? Could it be washed? Would it shrink or expand? Could it withstand hot water? What method of drying was required?

My rag bag in those days was filled with failed guesses: a shirt aged instantly in the wash, ten inches wider and four inches shorter; shrunken pants fit only for a Barbie doll; a sweater completely robbed of its nap; and a large furniture throw shriveled to a small, knobby square.

Printed care tags have become the determinants of my buying habits. If an item of clothing can't be tossed in the washer and dryer, it doesn't go in my shopping cart. If it has to be washed separately, it stays on the shelf. No wasteful single-item laundry allowed.

Holes as fashion statement

My mother kept a large wicker basket filled with items of clothing to be mended and socks to be darned. Early in my married life, I garnered a stack of my own. Then the magic occurred: holey became *holy* in the fashion world. If an item looked too new, it couldn't be worn. My teenagers favored old.

I walked past an upscale clothing shop last week. The window mannequins cavorted about, all dressed in shabby jeans. One pair of jeans was half torn at the knees; another had huge splotches and looked like someone had poured a bottle of bleach down the leg. I didn't see a pristine pair among them. No need for a mother ever to mend again.

Of course, I would never pay the price they were asking for those tattered togs. I know how to create my own: wear new jeans while doing some old-fashioned scrubbing on my hands and knees.

The Next Best Invention

Thinking about those best inventions of the last thirty years sent me off on a tangent. What innovation—not yet developed—could be a life-changer for housewives everywhere?

I want a GWDFP robot. This is a robot that does laundry—a gather, wash, dry, fold, and put-away model. I've already named him George. Possession of this machine would make me feel younger, more desirable, alluring, and charming. Well, not really—but it certainly would give me a free weekend and an empty laundry basket.

The specific mechanics of George elude my engineering skills, but I am confident that such an invention is not impossible. Just the other morning on TV, I glimpsed a demonstration of a robot performing miraculous feats in an operating room, leading me to conclude that folding clothes is hardly impossible for a man of steel.

George would look like a typical robot, but with extra-long arms to account for the stresses they would undergo. He would have color-sensitive digits. On any given morning, George would be programmed to roam the house, gathering up soiled and soggy items. He'd scoop dripping towels from the bathroom floor. Sensitivity to odors would help him find the wadded socks under the skirt of the couch and the cache of gym clothes under the bed.

He'd sort the dirty from the clean in the middle of each child's room. Then, with arms filled, he'd glide to the laundry area and deposit his load. One by one, he'd pass each item through his fingers, and he'd sort the colors. An extra joint on each digit would help him turn the socks— no more grass-filled, wrong-side-outs. George would then shake each item, ferreting out red crayons before they hit the dryer. Used tissues would never again be shredded in the dryer. A small metal detector built into his hand would discover chains, bolts, nails, and pins before they destroyed the washing machine motor. Then whiz, bang, clunk—he'd fill the washer and set the dial to start.

George would stand at ease, waiting patiently, monitoring his inferiors at their work. There would be no more squawking, off-balance machines. Next it would be creak, crack, click into the dryer.

When his underlings' tasks were complete, George would carry on. He'd embrace each item, familiarizing himself with scanned data: "White sock, size 8, Sally's room." He'd fold each item. Armed with piles of folded clothes, he'd cruise away, retracing his morning path, and then he would deposit the clean and dry apparel in the appointed drawers. At day's end, he'd cruise back to the laundry room faithfully to await another day.

The construction of George—such a scientific endeavor, with all its research and development—demands an accounting as to value, both present and future. Consider the endless possibilities. This invention could change the lives of millions. Everyone has laundry. Beyond the actual tasks he would perform, George could also impact some of our most urgent social problems. Take, for example, the problem of family breakdown. Consider the number of divorces that had this conversation as their precursor:

"Where in the #$%^& are my clean shorts?"

"Did you check the dryer?"

Silence. "Why can't you put them in my drawer?" Mutter. "Any idiot can do the laundry."

According to a recent poll, 99 percent of the male population agrees with this last statement. If any idiot can do laundry, why not a robot? Even in the most liberated households, where whiter than white is passé, folding is not.

Energy conservation is another major benefit. A robot that folds clothes as soon as the dryer shuts off would save countless kilowatts of energy. (Who among us hasn't sent the load for another spin when faced with crumpled clothes that have sagged for two hours after the dryer shut off?)

Best of all would be the impact on temperament. People everywhere would sing a sweeter tune. I see a mother in the midst of banquet preparations: potatoes to peel, roast to turn, vegetables to wash and pare, pies to bake, when her teenaged son bursts in the back door.

"Mom, Mom!" he shouts. "I need my baseball uniform washed and dried in half an hour!"

There would be no more screams of wrath, rage, and cursing her fate. Unruffled, she'd reply: "Let George do it." A Cheshire smile would follow.

Sup and Sew

The words "In my day . . ." were always a lead-in to my grandmother's tales. And here I am, repeating them.

In my day, every girl had to enroll in home economics classes. They consisted of a cooking class for half the year and a sewing class for the other half. I don't know when it was decided that these skills aren't necessary in a girl's education, but my daughter Lissy did not encounter this curriculum requirement.

I often find that what's stored in the cupboards of memory is capricious. My memories of cooking class are as vivid as if they took place last week. Perhaps it was the sight and taste of those not-quite-hard-boiled eggs swirled into a lumpy cream sauce in a most unappetizing way that locked them in my mind.

We girls (note the sexist educational requirement) were divided into teams of four with no regard for skill level. As one of six children, I'd been cooking and helping my mother in the kitchen for years. It wasn't so with most of my classmates. For some of them, learning to boil water was not just a wisecrack, but an actual skill to be acquired. Our output was mediocre at best. We were required to eat what we cooked without complaint. (Bathroom trips to throw up were not an option.)

My team did manage to produce hot, flaky biscuits. In spite of our less-than-gourmet products, I liked that class. I still have our recipe for meatloaf. We had an enthusiastic, good-natured young teacher whom we admired. Unfortunately this was not the case with the sewing teacher.

The sewing instructor was a grim-faced older woman, with steel-gray hair wound tightly in a bun at the crown of her head. Back then I was sure she lacked a sense of humor. She rarely smiled or relaxed. Perhaps she did have a quirky sense of humor, though. The last project she assigned us was the crafting of a dirndl skirt. Each student—regardless of size or build—had to make that skirt and wear it in a style show. The skirts consisted of yards of fabric gathered onto a waistband. Only a pencil-thin waif looks good in a dirndl—anyone else looks like a beer barrel. Was it simply a joke on her part?

The dirndl was a harbinger of things to come in my sewing future. It is impossible to assess the fit and feel of a garment with only a tissue pattern and a bolt of cloth. This deficiency is now being tackled with the help of virtual bodies on computers, but nothing really substitutes for the finished product on a flesh-and-blood body. Mistakes in the construction of a garment are difficult—if not impossible—to fix.

Before underpaid workers in foreign countries made most clothing, many women fashioned their own garments as a way to save money. I tried. Again, memory is fickle. I associate sewing with frustration and error. If you're cooking with young children in the house, it's possible to involve them as participants. Sewing is a solitary occupation. I quickly learned to attempt sewing projects only when the children were in bed. Even the solitude was no guarantee of perfection. I once cut out a lovely navy blue, polka dot dress only to discover that I had cut two right sleeves and had run out of fabric to correct my mistake. Another time I sewed through my own finger with the sewing machine, necessitating a tetanus shot. (It gave the expression "all sewed up" an entirely new meaning.) While fashioning a blue linen Easter coat for Lissy, I made tailored button-holes on the wrong front placket.

My error list goes on. Finally I reached a point in life where I donated my sewing machine to the Goodwill store with the fondest of farewells. From then on, I sent minor sewing projects to the tailor at the dry cleaning shop.

Not only are our own memories quirky; family memories aren't synchronized either. Recently, after a Saturday morning walk, Jay burst in the door, eager to share some good news with me.

"You'll never guess what I found at a garage sale." He proceeded to display a neat green-and-white case. His eyes sparkled. "A sewing machine for only seven dollars. What a bargain!"

I eyed it with feigned interest. "Will you need help threading the needle?" I asked.

TRIAL BY FAMILY

I suffer from Associative Identity Disorder—my association with certain people brings out an entirely new pattern of perception and interaction.

At different times, I've been an entertainer, nurse, cop, teacher, taxi driver, and dietician.

"Please," I pleaded with my four-year-old, "just eat four peas—they're like birthday candles. It's like a vitamin for every year."

He glared at the dreaded green balls on his plate. "If I do, I'll throw up."

Our Train Trip

I predicted the demise of train travel years before it actually happened. Jay and I decided to take our two preschoolers on a train trip to Seattle, boarding the train in Bismarck, North Dakota.

The train had a Vista dome and the views would be spectacular. Our departure was pleasant. At that time, trains were not suitable for crawling children. The berths were too narrow and the food was beyond the budget of young couples, but the views outside the windows were marvelous. We whizzed up and down mountains and in between snow-covered trees. The sun dazzled on the clear, crisp landscape.

Seattle was ahead of its time. The World's Fair had provided the impetus for the development of childcare facilities that could accommodate visitors. Our hotel had competent, reliable babysitters.

Jay and I conventioned for three days. Up until then, everything went according to schedule. On Thursday night, we crawled into bed after the final banquet and tour of the city. The next morning, my cousin was due to pick us up and take us to her home in one of the ski resort areas for a few more days of vacation.

That morning at 2:11 a.m., our two-year-old, Danny, erupted with a cry followed by a gurgling sound. It wasn't sufficient warning—he threw up before we could get to him. We bathed him, washed the soiled bedsheet in the sink, and dried it with towels. The other sheet had been spared, so we spread it out on a clean spot. By 3:00 a.m. we attempted to get back to sleep.

"Arwwwk!" Jeff, our four-year-old, was the next to spout vomit. I fumbled for the light. It was 3:23 a.m. He managed to include Danny in his target area. Two baths were in order, along with more laundry in the sink.

By 6:00 a.m., we'd repeated this procedure with each of the children. The smell in our room was enough to asphyxiate us. Being sick at home is unpleasant; being sick in a hotel room is impossible.

"We're heading home!" Jay announced. He phoned the train station to see when we could get on a train. We made a second call to my cousin. She volunteered to drive in the thirty miles and take us to the station.

By 11:30 a.m., we had hugged hello and goodbye and deposited sick kids, the luggage, and ourselves in a little compartment on the train.

The train was beginning to chug and jerk out of the station when Jay said, "We forgot to get cash."

My upbringing had included a very stern warning: "Never travel with more cash than you can afford to lose." At that time in our lives, ten dollars was about the limit.

"Count your money." Jay said, with an element of discouragement. (Remember, I was the one with three cents in my pocket on our honeymoon.)

Between us we had $32.84. Jay shrugged. "We'll have to put our meals on the credit card."

Our two boys were prostrate, even refusing water. We headed for the dining car, where we ordered toast and bowls of clear soup. The boys barely ate.

As we made our way out of the diner, Jay stopped. "I'd better check with the steward." He gestured to one. "Do you accept American Express?"

The steward's face was impassive. "No, sir."

Jay shrugged. "We'll have to give you a check."

"We don't accept checks."

"What do you mean, you don't accept checks? We paid for our train tickets with a check."

The steward's face was inscrutable, as he looked straight through us. "That's a different department."

Back in our compartment, we mapped out our strategy. Our cash had dwindled to less than twenty dollars. We were glad, at least, that the boys wouldn't suffer. They had no appetites.

If anything is quicker than a child's sickness, it's his recovery. By eight o'clock the next morning, the boys had not only recovered—they were ravenous, which they declared in dramatic tones. We guided them down the aisle to the next car. Breakfast was being served at a snack bar. The boys climbed up on stools, and Jay and I sat on either side of them. Jay looked over the menu and made quick calculations.

"How about a bowl of oatmeal, boys? You don't want to eat too much after being sick." He looked over at me. "Coffee for us."

The waiter took our order, and in minutes, the boys were eating steaming bowls of oatmeal. Jeff finished his in two minutes flat.

"I want another bowlful," he declared, licking his lips.

"Shhh." I leaned over. "We don't get seconds on the train."

"But I'm hungry! I want another bowl," my thin, blond, big-eyed child pleaded.

The waiter stood in front of us. His eyes maintained an imperious glaze, but he had seen Jeff. "Would you like to order?"

"No, thank you," we demurred.

Jeff turned his large eyes toward his father. "But I am *starving*."

"No, son, you're *not* starving." Jay spoke quietly, in a measured tone.

Jeff was undeterred. "I want another bowl of oatmeal."

The waiter stood there.

Jay leaned over the table toward Danny. "Finish up so we can go back to the Vista dome."

Jeff tried a new tactic and directly addressed the waiter. "I want another bowl of oatmeal."

The waiter looked at Jay who refused to meet his eyes. I concentrated on my coffee cup. The man shrugged. "Why don't I give him another bowl—no extra charge?"

Jeff lapped it up.

"No more trips to the dining car," Jay declared, counting the change in his pocket.

We survived the rest of the day on two packages of beer nuts, one sandwich, and soda for the boys.

We arrived in Bismarck at eleven-thirty that night. Jay carried one boy; I carried the other. An aging porter lugged our four suitcases off the train. He set the bags down on the platform. Jay fumbled in his pocket and handed the man a coin.

"I'm sorry. It's all I have."

The poor man stood, staring down at the thin dime in his hand.

We headed for the nearest restaurant displaying an American Express emblem and ordered the biggest steaks on the menu.

Silence Is . . .

Children should be seen and not heard is a discredited adage. Enlightened by psychologists of the past few decades, parents now encourage their offspring to speak up—to make their thoughts known and their voices heard. I subscribe to this tolerant point of view for a number of reasons. For example, I've found silence to be a harbinger of impending disaster.

One morning I was working in the kitchen, keeping one ear alert for the boys (ages two and four), who were playing downstairs. My other ear was tuned to the radio on the counter beside me. I was busy mixing bread dough in preparation for cinnamon rolls, humming along with the radio.

It was a bright, cozy day. The sun shimmered on the snow banks outside the kitchen window. It looked as if the snow had been sprinkled with glitter for a party. I kneaded the dough with strong, even strokes and formed it into two large balls. My pans were lined up on the counter, already layered with brown sugar, white syrup, butter, and pecans, awaiting the circles of dough.

We were living in a small, wood-framed house with a full basement. The basement was empty except for a furnace, a washer and dryer, and a laundry chute where dirty clothes tumbled down from the bathroom.

The basement had a clean, concrete floor. It was the perfect play space in cold, icy winters. It was here that the boys kept their tricycles, Tonka trucks, a green army play-Jeep, wooden blocks, and large packing boxes. They also had a set of cardboard, shoebox-sized blocks that were painted to look like bricks.

The wooden vertical support columns made perfect roadway poles. Most mornings the boys rode their tricycles in loops and turns, careening around the basement in high spirits. They built forts with the boxes and red blocks. Sometimes they drove their vehicles into these structures with smashing results.

I began rolling a ball of dough on a wooden breadboard and stopped in midhum. Complete silence issued from below. I cocked my head, both ears fully tuned to the lower region of the house. I abandoned the dough, washed and dried my hands, and set off to investigate this absence of noise. The thud of my shoes on the maroon-painted wooden steps announced my approaching arrival. The boys were crouched by one of the support columns. Two little faces looked up at me across the expanse. They were safe.

I breathed a sigh of relief. They abandoned their positions, hopped on their tricycles again, and began looping a course around the basement perimeter. They were a little too quick in their surrender, so I set off across the floor to investigate.

As I neared the column, I saw that it sported a new floral design. I sucked in a breath and dropped to my knees to get a closer look. A napkin from a wedding gift set—a yellow and green floral design matching my yellow linen tablecloth—was nailed to the wooden column. I retrieved a hammer from Jay's toolbox and began pulling out the nails, counting as I worked.

" . . . twenty-nine, thirty . . . "

Then I gasped. Below the impaled napkin was a newly sawed cut. It had been made with a toy saw, but had made quite an impression. I envisioned the house shifting above us.

"Boys!" What was it those psychologists said?

Shopping

"We'll do it quickly—just whip in and out of the store," my mother coaxed. Shopping with three children in tow was never my idea of a quick trip. "I want you to help pick out a wedding gift for Marnie. I'll help with the children."

I relented. We washed the children's faces, and Mother herded the boys to the car while I folded the stroller and strapped Lissy into her car seat. In a few minutes we were at the shopping center, in the china department at Macy's. My bravado faltered as I surveyed the scene. Table after table stretched before us, each set with sparkling crystal and china in patterns of gold and silver. Each piece was covered with varied and intricate designs. Sterling silver pieces complemented each setting. My two boys stood beside me, unimpressed.

"You two stay by Grandma!" I commanded. "This will only take a few minutes."

Lissy sat in her stroller like a cherub in her pink bonnet and lacy white dress.

"I think Marnie's patterns are registered," Mother remarked. "I'll take the boys and go check." They set off to look for the bridal registry.

"No running, boys!" I called after them.

I shook my head. The thought of letting those two loose in a china department required suspension of my better judgment. I meandered through the aisles, pushing Lissy's stroller. The floral arrangements on the tables were lovely. I began to dream a little. Candles and fresh linens were only in my dreams in those days.

Mother began heading toward me. "I found Marnie's entry in the . . . " Her voice stopped. I stared at her. She clasped a hand to her chest, and her eyes widened. She gasped.

"Mom?"

She gestured wildly at Lissy. I dropped my gaze. Lissy was leaning forward in her stroller, one little arm reaching out in front of her. She had the corner of a linen tablecloth held tightly in her fist, and she was pulling. A gold-edged goblet teetered.

"Lissy," I whispered hoarsely. I dropped to my knees, a supplicant. "Here. Mommy will help you." I attempted a smile.

I moved my hands toward her slowly, then got her hand in my grasp. I pried her fist open, one tiny finger at a time. The cloth dropped free. Mother steadied the crystal.

"Ohhhhhh!" My breath escaped in relief. Mother and I stared at each other. "You're on your own, Mom." I beckoned to the boys, and we flew out of the store.

Emergency Room Visits

"**Y**our mother's that gray-haired lady," I overheard Mark's friend say.

It's true—I have a lot of gray hair. When confronted with gray hair, some people pluck out the offenders; or, in the case of too many (plucking would denude them), they color the evidence. I don't. I wear my gray hair as a badge. I've earned every strand of it. Visits to the emergency room inspired their share of them.

Life is a booby trap when you're two years old. For some children, the age of two lasts a long time.

Few things are more humiliating to a parent than a trip to the emergency room. It is a public declaration of failure. You have failed to protect your child. Never mind that he was visiting Aunt Helen at the time, or playing football at the Y. You berate yourself: "I should have been there."

One of the by-products of parenting is that it keeps you aware of your humanity. After all, we are mere, fallible mortals. I've been reminded of my mortality—and my children's—too often.

When my children were preschoolers, I saw so much of our pediatrician that he and I could have been suspected of having an affair, had I not always had a child in tow. The physician and I had a mutual interest—keeping my children alive and well. I had a baby and a two-year-old. One Wednesday the two-year-old stair-stepped up the kitchen drawers in order to reach the highest shelf above. Then he crammed a fistful of iron tablets in his mouth. I caught him just in time to swab out a handful of them. Since I was uncertain if I had gotten them all, we made that trip to emergency room.

The following Wednesday, he found an old tube of model airplane glue crammed into a crack in the basement wall, which necessitated another trip to the emergency room. As I sobbed on the phone to Dr. Jack, bemoaning these excursions, I wailed, "What am I going to do?"

He wryly responded, "*Next* Wednesday I'd watch him."

Eventually we moved to another city. On a return visit to our hometown, I called Dr. Jack to update him about a foot problem he had treated for one of the boys. He ended our conversation with the polite remark: "If I can do anything for you while you're in town, just give me a call." Foolish man.

Two nights later, at two in the morning, I rang him. "Jeff has fallen out of a top bunk bed and split his chin open." We were off to the emergency room.

Once you arrive at an emergency room, you discover that emergencies have degrees. The gaping gash spouting quarts of blood is only a minor wound. Then there are the forms, and the wait for an empty cubicle to hide in. One year I capped my Mother's Day celebration with a three-hour visit to the emergency room. A child's spill from a bicycle had resulted in a concussion.

The ministry of healing in the emergency room has never elicited the proper response from my children. When they were small and had cuts stitched or stomachs pumped, they were wrapped mummy-style by attendants. Jeff fought this confinement so hard that he ruptured tiny blood vessels in his face. He looked like he had measles by the time we left the hospital. Danny's reaction was even more explicit. He fell and split the back of his head open, and his treatment had been received under protest. When we were ready to be dismissed, I carried my screaming, kicking monster to the door. The intern who had done the stitching followed and stepped ahead of us to open the door. I paused a moment to shout over the howling: "Thank you."

Danny halted his yelling. He reached across my chest and with his little hand balled into a fist, planted a blow on the doctor's arm. So much for gratitude!

Surviving Half-Staff

"Life with Father" was an old radio program. The modern version is "Life without Father" followed by "What Happens When Dad's Away."

First the children get sick. Our pediatrician had been a Navy doctor in New England. According to him, it was a fact that when the ships went out, the kids came in. At our house we suffered through tonsillitis, chicken pox, ear infections, cuts, bruises, contusions, and other ailments, all with Jay consoling us from a long distance.

Next the weather gets bad. The absence of fathers is one indicator of weather completely overlooked by scientists. While I am not a meteorologist, this clue enabled me to predict the advent of floods, blizzards, tornadoes, hail storms, and ice storms. The occurrence of these freaks of nature always took place when Jay was out of town. (Another predictive phenomenon is also common knowledge among mothers: snowstorms necessitating school closings always occur at the end of long Christmas holidays. Sometimes the closure doesn't even require the white stuff. One year we had no snow—only a record-breaking cold spell that required the schools to close the morning after Christmas break.)

Our midwestern city was hit with a flood of such magnitude that it should occur only once in five hundred years, according to the weather bureau. Jay was in Europe at the time. (We had a similar flood two years later. Time flies.) A March snowstorm blew in with surprising speed and little forewarning when Jay was on a business trip to Minneapolis. The two older boys were preschoolers and I was pregnant with Lissy. The wind howled and huffed, flailing at us all night. In the morning, I looked out the kitchen window. The house next door had disappeared. The only thing visible was snow—blinding, raging, driving snow. According to the battery-operated radio, it was a blizzard.

It had been warm in bed. Now that the boys and I were up, we were cold. We bundled up in winter coats, scarves, and boots. The electricity was off, rendering the furnace useless. I promised myself I'd keep a stiff upper lip. (This was easy, considering I had a stiff, frozen upper body.) We'd make an adventure of it. If only we had a fireplace, I thought. I later discovered (in another blizzard) that a fireplace is of little use in heating a house. It's like those old-fashioned toasters; only the side of your body next to the fire stays warm.

The boys joined in the adventure. Thick mittens made it difficult to play with their toys, but they managed. We did well until I noticed the dog shivering with cold. Time to abandon ship! The radio rallied us. Residents without electricity would be rescued by the National Guard and taken to a temporary shelter. Our phone was still operating. I called the emergency number, and men in uniform soon arrived to escort us to the house next door. Our neighbors had a propane kitchen stove. They lit the burners and the oven, closed off part of the house, and welcomed us in. We got a phone call from Jay while we were there. The telephone operator had tracked us down—one of the benefits of living in a small town.

Another time we managed a double whammy while Jay was away—chicken pox and a blizzard. I can still remember the feeling of rescue when Jay—looking like a snow monster—arrived home at four-thirty in the morning. With all the major airports closed, he'd caught a train from Chicago. A police car had driven him from the train station to within a couple blocks of our house. Unable to get closer, he'd waded through waist-high snow the final two blocks.

By the time we experienced the tornado, our family had doubled in size. The sirens began blowing at about two in the afternoon. It was summertime, so all four children were at home. This time Jay was not far away—he was simply trapped in his office downtown. We had lived in tornado country for a long time, so everyone knew the routine. We fled for the basement and hid under the pool table near the windowless wall (backed by an earthen mound). It was there that four kids, two dogs and I waited out the storm. Simply keeping everyone corralled under the table was its own kind of disaster, but we survived the pool table crunch and the storm.

Other challenges have occurred with Jay away: a huge, coiled snake sunning itself on the warm front stoop and the dog dying from an accidental poisoning.

Sometimes when I look back on these trials, I marvel at the changes modernization has wrought. My parents spent few nights apart in their decades of married life. My farmer father was tied to home by crops and cattle. The cows had to be milked morning and evening.

Do benefits accrue from all these traumas with just mom at the helm? I think of it now as survival training for us. The children and I are stronger, more independent, and more self-assured. We shoveled the driveway; we cleaned up debris; we mopped up water. It's like that old method of learning to swim—toss the student into the water and he or she either sinks or swims. Still, when Jay finally appeared on the scene—like a ninth-inning pitcher—the sight of him was a welcome relief.

LUNCH PAILS AND GYM SHORTS

*The joy I felt the first morning I sent all four children out
the door to school was soon tempered by having to clean*

*up after a sick dog. It's an attendant law of child-rearing—
the seesaw rule of equilibrium.*

*My college chemistry classes left me with little appe-
tite for (or knowledge of) that basic science. I listened to
lectures with three hundred other students, followed by a
lab taught in a portable tinderbox classroom by a verbally-
challenged introvert.*

*Other college classes eliminated whatever remaining
interest I may have had in applied sciences; shepherding
four children through the ritual called "Science Fair" is
my definition of hell.*

I Don't Volunteer

Once I volunteered to supervise Mark's class on a field trip to the zoo. The day before the event, I stepped in a hole at the golf course and tore all the ligaments in my foot. What some people do to get out of volunteering!

However, the reason I don't volunteer is that it is unnecessary. I reared children who volunteer me on my behalf.

"Could anyone bring cookies?"

Lissy's hand waves wildly in the air. "My mother will do it!"

"Who'd like to drive for our field trip?"

Danny's hand pops up. "My mother."

I worked hard to break them of this nasty habit.

To be perfectly serious, I have strong convictions about volunteering. I say, "Take your turn."

As long as the world expects after-school activities to be provided by volunteers, everyone needs to share the work. I've heard the feeble excuse, "I just don't have the talent for it." That's bunkum. Most volunteer jobs require less than perfection. The magic ingredient is time.

I've also heard the worn-out excuse: "I work." People who rely on this excuse need to realize that *everybody* works. It's a matter of scheduling priorities. If you believe in extracurricular activities for children, you should be part of the "extra."

Another worn-out excuse for refusing to volunteer is a lack of talent for crafts. I've found that if you have zero talent for crafts, you can substitute enthusiasm. It will carry the day. Attack projects with vigor. Show these children how *not* to do something by displaying your sorry, drooping project. Every child will then recognize that he or she can do a better job than you. Begin the school year by letting parents know that you are not one of those volunteer leaders who devote themselves to sending home beautiful projects. Your focus is to let Rory do it by himself.

I have been a den mother, a Brownie leader, a choir mother, and a room mother. It's an enriching experience. Well, if it's not enriching, it's enlightening.

The year that I was a Cub Scout den mother I discovered that it always rains on Wednesdays. For thirty-six weeks, I cleaned out the garage every Wednesday afternoon so that we could have our den meeting inside.

Volunteering has highlighted one of life's mysteries for me: Why is it that some of the loveliest people have the worst kids? Ask any choir mother, den leader, or scoutmaster the same question. The worst children always have perfect attendance as well. (Now that's no mystery. Challenging children get dumped off at meetings so that they can bug somebody else for an hour.)

Volunteering contributes to acting ability. As a choir mother marshaling a group of Pilgrims and Indians to the altar for a Thanksgiving service, I discovered one of the more trying boys had torn off three children's paper collars and pointed hats. Our Pilgrim population was being decimated. I cracked a serene smile, grasped his shirt until

I could feel skin, and led the offender to a spot behind the cross.

"If you don't behave, I'll march you straight down the aisle to your parents," I hissed. Then I sedately led him back to the altar. God forgives volunteers.

Volunteers learn to conquer their fears. I rode the Sky Ride in a flimsy metal bucket with Brenda and Amy because their mothers had sent notes requiring that a leader accompany them. For that reason, even though I am terrified of heights, I had to dangle high above the ground as Brenda and Amy hung over the edges of the basket, hair flying, feet kicking, and arms flailing. I clung to them shouting: "Don't rock the bucket!"

Shared leadership promotes great friendships. It's the psychological phenomenon that says, "We're in this together." Sally and I co-led a group of Brownies. For our spring project—Mother's Day, May Day, and Happy-to-Be-Alive Day—our Brownies made pastel string baskets. The project seemed simple enough. We read the directions, bought the supplies, prepared Sally's kitchen, and forged ahead. The project required each child to blow up a balloon and then wind string around the balloon to form a basket. We used multicolored crochet thread for the baskets. The secret to these creations is that in order to hold its shape, the string must first be dipped in sugar water. Once the basket dries, the balloon can be popped and the basket cut to shape a handle. It is then ready to be filled with delights.

The instructions for these projects never seem to include the little tips that would help prepare you for the aftermath. By the time our troop of girls had dipped and dripped yards of sugary string, Sally's kitchen was the equivalent of two-sided tape. No matter what surface you touched, you stuck. We had covered every flat surface with newspaper, but this only added to the mess. Sticky papier-mâché adhered to every surface. We washed down her entire kitchen in an attempt to rid it of adhesive. The experience served as a catalyst for its own set of inside jokes—with allusions to a "sweet project," "one you can really stick with," and "one the girls can get all wrapped up in." This is how friendships develop.

That is the magic lesson behind volunteering. Adults form fast friendships through volunteering, and they provide excellent role models for the children. Children mimic the actions of the adults around them. If they see that adults find ways to accommodate each other, compromise, and accept others' ideas—all while enjoying their small charges and each other—this is the best lesson of all.

So Johnny
Wants to Cook

I know a man with a master's degree who needs someone to fry his egg. Ridiculous! If you can read, you can cook.

I launched myself into a cooking class with this resolute statement as an inspiration. I was a college student at the time, doing group work in a community center. My pupils were girls aged eight to ten. The statement at the top of the page still stands, but time and experience have added a few amendments. What are the basics—the how, when, where, and why—of teaching anyone how to cook?

Begin simply. I bought a cookbook and found myself with ten little girls clustered around me at a center-island counter in an oversized, institutional kitchen. The girls were eager and expectant. Their faces glowed. I remembered my home economics cooking classes and eating the creamed, half-cooked eggs, and I wasn't quite as enthusiastic. For our first project, I decided that biscuits would be an easy task. We measured flour and added baking powder and salt. I turned to an eager girl at my elbow.

"Get me the shortening."

She blinked and stared at me. "Huh?"

"The shortening," I repeated.

Then, gazing into her face, it dawned on me. From her point of view, shortening had more to do with distance than with biscuits. Thus my first amendment was added. If you can read *and figure out what the words mean*, you can cook.

I soon discovered that poring over the cookbook and dreaming of exotic concoctions was a major part of any project. We plunged ahead, buoyed by the girls' exuberance and my inexperience.

Those girls and I shared many experiences. Once we made a spectacular layer cake (from the perspective of eight-year-olds). The child who carried the finished product from the counter to the table managed to trip and dump it upside-down in the middle of the brown, pitted, linoleum floor. Ten pairs of eyes settled on me, waiting for a cue. One pair had big teardrops forming in the corners. I brushed aside my prior complaints about janitorial service in the building. I carefully lifted the cake off the floor, scraping at its edges.

"It will still taste good!" I declared. We devoured every bit.

My first experiences of cooking with children were with other people's children in other people's kitchens. This was easier. It was preparation for the day that I had four children of my own. Teaching how to cook requires demonstration, patience, and paper towels. If you are short on something, don't let it be the paper towels.

One of the basic cooking skills is cracking an egg. I was teaching my son Danny. I gave him careful instructions: "Wash it first. Then tap the egg on the edge of the counter and crack it. Pull the shell apart and let it plop into the cup."

Danny grabbed an egg and rinsed it. Kawham! He cracked it on the edge of the cupboard, and it splattered on the kitchen floor. This is where paper towels come in handy. They're perfect for cleaning up a slimy egg.

I gave amended instructions. "Tap gently!"

In the first stage of cooking, when children are learning the basics, they are meticulous to a fault. Any project takes forever. The second stage is more experimental. I call it the purple frosting stage.

"Why did you dump it all together? It says, 'Step one: cream shortening and sugar.'"

"I wanted to see what would happen."

"There's something unique about these cookies." I attempted to bite into one of the strange-looking flat rocks.

"I thought I'd try something new."

Don't ask what.

In this second stage, children willingly pedal to the grocery store for rare spices. They're excited about any unusual undertakings. My brother and I created the only pigeon pie I've ever eaten at this point in my cooking career. Experiment leads to discovery: only fathers fully appreciate such delicacies as pigeon pie.

Eventually children grow beyond this second stage. They still partake in experiments, but on a modified scale. They develop an appreciation for visual appeal. They tire of weird colors and textures and, from their lofty new perspective, critically examine a younger brother's green peanut butter mixture.

Where do you teach kids to cook? The answer is not as obvious as you might think.

"I taught my daughter to cook via telephone." An interviewer was quoting a female executive in our city.

The idea intrigued me—she had a point. When I thought about teaching my pupils in the kitchen, I had to agree it was probably safer via telephone. Even simple projects can become disastrous.

One evening I sat with eyes half-open as Danny poured the ingredients for instant chocolate pudding into the blender. He pushed the button on the blender, and I shot out of my chair.

"Turn it off!" I shouted.

Driven by the whirlwind in the blender, chocolate pudding flew everywhere, peppering our clothes, speckling cupboard doors, and slicking up the kitchen floor. Danny's face was covered with the chocolate mess.

"I don't think you had the lid on tight enough," I murmured, as we wiped up with paper towels. Six months later, I was still finding spots of dried pudding in cracks and corners.

Experiences such as this served to emphasize another commandment: "Clean up after yourselves."

This rule has a dual purpose. It not only aids the instructor; it has a tempering effect on the pupil. A dream is coupled with reality when a child gazes at a two-page recipe in a cookbook, drooling and savoring, and then asks: "How many pans does it take?"

The third stage of children's cooking is the most satisfying. It answers the question: "Why bother?" I knew the whole process was worthwhile when Lissy said, "You can just sit down, Mother. I'll fix you a cheese omelet for lunch." The entrée was a lovely, golden offering.

Cooking has always been a favorite activity of those who work with children. It contains built-in teaching devices. Cooking is an activity that requires planning and demands completion. It inspires creativity. It provides immediate satisfaction for a job well done. Children who learn to cook gain independence, preparing to go out and fend for themselves. It's vital preparation for growing up.

Working together taught us more than cooking. Years after I had picked up that child's cake from the floor, Jeff baked a layer cake. To be helpful, I moved it from the stove to the counter . . . and dumped it upside down.

He stared at me, and I prepared myself for a barrage of words. He rose to the occasion, picking chocolate pieces off the floor.

"It'll still taste good!" he said—and we devoured it.

Lingo and
Language — 4COL

Some days family life is like watching a movie in which the sound does not coordinate with the picture. You can see mouths moving, but you have no idea what is being said.

It's not the generation gap or the idioms. Every decade's teenagers have their favorite slang expressions. Parents soon learn the meaning of such phrases: Cool! Awesome! Dorky! Glam! It's a snap catching on to this jargon. It's not even the acronyms, 4COL (for crying out loud). Any parent can pick up a glossary of these terms.

It's perspective, vantage point, and frame of reference. It's as if you and your offspring are living on separate space stations. The two worlds coexist, but unlike those proverbial ships passing in the night, the children in their own space are oblivious to ours.

"There's nothing to eat." I hear this comment just after I finish shelving $150.00 worth of groceries.

I see my daughter mope at the kitchen table, propping her chin on her hand. "There's nothing to do around here." I peer at her over five baskets of unfolded laundry.

"Nobody's home." This pronouncement comes from a child who's looking you straight in the eye.

"Since you're not doing anything . . . " This comment comes from a child addressing a parent engaged in a Sunday afternoon nap.

The most blatant examples of our total failure in communication occurred one weekend. Two kids were sprawled on the floor with the television blaring a football game. The CD player blatted out a rap beat above the whirring of the mixer (Jeff was baking cookies). A fourth child was working on a project with enamel paint, newspapers covering the kitchen table. The dog howled at the patio door; he wanted to paint as well. Jay and I plotted our escape from this bedlam. Unpaid bills demanded our attention. It would be the perfect time to head for the desk downstairs.

"We're looking for peace and quiet," I announced.

We beat it for the lower regions. Once seated at the table, we dumped the files and began to sort, heads bent over our work. Somewhere in my subconscious mind, I heard the door open and the patter of feet on the stairs.

Kawoosh! Danny swept by on his skateboard, crouched low, merrily mouthing conversation as he sailed by.

"Peace!" I screamed. "Peace and quiet!"

Danny stopped short. "Oh."

The problem was much more severe than I suspected.

I'll Take a Teenager Any Day

I'll take a teenager any day. I've heard a lot of complaining about this age group, but believe me—they're the pick of the lot when it comes to visits to the pediatrician, allergist, pedodontist, and orthodontist.

I've had ample opportunity to compare babies, preschoolers, preadolescents, and teenagers, and I'll take older kids any day. Only last week, as I sat in the dentist's office with my teenaged boys, I offered a prayer of thanksgiving for them. I'm past the age when they explore, scream, kick, whine, cry, and wail in the outer office.

Waiting for the appointed hour in our dentist's office is like being banished to someone's closet with the neighborhood children thrown in. The office is about ten by fourteen and outlined with furniture. The center of the room is heaped with toys. One wall is covered with huge pictures of aquatic life; another wall is papered with a frenzy of circus scenes. The water scenes tranquilize the mothers, and the circus images pep up the children.

On this particular day, the dentist was running forty minutes late and lagging. Three mothers with nine children filled the tiny office. In the middle of the room, two preschool siblings were playing with large wooden blocks.

Each one punctuated every move with a slap at the other: "Mine!" One soon dissolved into tears and ran to bury his face in a woman's shoulder. Her identity betrayed, she had to claim these two. This mother was a picture of pained patience, wearing a thin smile.

"Let's share, boys." She arched an eyebrow at me and shook her head. Danny let out an extended sigh. I was comfortably smug.

In the first dozen years with my children, we went through weekly allergy shots, ear infections, tubes in the ears, braces on the teeth, braces on legs, stitches three times on the same chin, stitches in the head, stomachs pumped, and enough tonsillitis to result in two tonsillectomies. Through all this trauma was the purgatory of the waiting room.

I was totally unprepared for the phase of parenthood that takes place in the waiting room.

My first two children were boys and, without reflecting on their characters, I can tell you that they were active. Somehow by the time I had cleaned and dressed them, dressed myself, packed a tote bag full of surprises, recleaned them, and towed them to the doctor's office, I looked forward to a quiet wait. An hour of sedate sitting would have been welcome. Not with my boys!

I kept placating myself by saying, "Bright children are curious." If this adage is true, my children were brilliant. They played hide-and-seek around the chairs, belly-crawled under the couches, and inspected the green plants in the corners. An artificial orange tree stood by the door in our pediatrician's office, conspicuous and inviting. I always kept one eye on it, wondering which one of the boys would be the first to pluck a plastic orange. They merely squeezed.

The room had two small chairs tucked under a child-sized table that displayed an assortment of children's books and magazines. The furnishings were decorative, but the children ignored them. The boys would leaf through the adult magazines—a dilapidated collection of outdated white elephants—as they hopped in and out of the vinyl-covered chairs.

Some of my contemporaries contentedly let their off-spring explore while they sat reading placidly. I could never hypnotize myself into this relaxed state. I perched on my chair in a state of expectation, anticipating catastrophe at any moment. My instinct did not go unrewarded.

Eventually we'd be ushered from the waiting room to a postage stamp-sized examining room where we'd spend another half-hour. It was like going from a closet to a toy box—without the toys. Crammed into this tiny space with no other form of amusement, I became the obligatory entertainer. I unzipped my tote bag and began my routine.

"Mommy will read you this nice book."

"How about a graham cracker, boys?"

I'd sing, dance, weigh and measure each child, wash their hands, and guard the colored vials that tempted tiny fingers.

Without fail I'd have my hand on the doorknob, ready to stalk out and never return, when rescue presented itself in the form of the beaming doctor. "Well, who's sick today?"

So I count my blessings, grateful that my children have reached the age where they disdainfully eye the younger ones engaged in waiting room antics. Later in the car, my boys murmur to each other: "Geesh, did you see what awful kids that lady had?"

I'll take these teenagers any day. I'll claim them all as mine. Now I discover I've come full cycle in the process as they slouch in chairs on the opposite side of the waiting room, their eyes averted from my motherly glances. They pretend they're not with me.

"It's too embarrassing, Mom!"

Sweet Sixteen
(with Coda)

Sweet sixteen is a phrase coined by greeting card companies. Parents have a totally different take on it.

When your child turns sixteen, you join a club of parents commiserating with each other and bracing themselves for the inevitable. Lecturing becomes part of your daily routine. I have no reservations about letting youth test their wings. That's what parenting is all about—preparing them to leave the nest and to be independent. When it comes to trying their wheels, it's a different matter. No other event in the lives of parents and children is as divisive in terms of *us* and *them* as that first driver's license. Even though it's a step toward adulthood, parents approach it with terrible fear and a huge sense of lost control. Teenagers welcome it with impatience, reflecting their intense desire to be on their own. Mothers are notorious for their reactions to the student driver—they go berserk. The advent of a teenaged driver heralds a whole new set of sleep-deprived nights.

My driving lecture began with the phrase: "Driving is a big responsibility."

This was followed by observations about the miserable skills of the majority of drivers on the road. It ended with,

"Just remember—neither your father nor I have ever had an accident."

When our first teenager began driving, I was lulled into a false sense of security by a few uneventful weeks. Then one evening, I received a call. Jeff was late for work. Did I know where he was? Of course, I told myself—he had run out of gas. His gas tank had never known the comfort of fullness.

I headed out to find him, searching the streets for a figure toting a gas can. An hour later, without finding him, I headed home and pulled into the drive. Jeff's car was there. My heart sank to my shoes when I saw the driver's side of the car caved in, a mangled mess. Jeff appeared in the doorway, safe.

"Was anyone hurt?" I swallowed my sobs.

He shook his head, a worried look in his eyes. "What d'ya think Dad will say?"

"He'll be thankful you're safe. What happened?"

"I was making a turn and didn't see this car. Can you drive me to work?"

My husband accepted the wrecked car with an admirable equanimity. "Thank God no one was hurt. Anyone can make a mistake," he said, as he inspected the damage.

The next day he confessed to me, "I got a ticket myself yesterday—for running a red light I didn't see."

I consoled him. "Fathers aren't supposed to be perfect."

Jeff parked his damaged car at the far end of the drive to await the insurance inspection. That afternoon I raced out to my car, hurrying to make my pickup at the school. I turned the ignition key and began to back up.

Crunch! I gasped. I pulled forward. Another metallic noise! I jumped out of my car. I'd hit Jeff's car and, in pulling forward, I'd bent my car's bumper into an L-shape. I called Jeff and his friend to help me get the bumper into drivable condition.

"Mom, you've been telling me what a good driver you are," Jeff remarked. "You forget to check your mirror?"

I knew I had it coming. Everyone's allowed one mistake.

The insurance company declared Jeff's car totaled, and he bought his second car. I made an appointment to have the bumper on my car replaced. Life returned to normal.

Jeff parked his car at the end of the drive. I raced to make my pickup at school.

Crunch! I shut my eyes, pulled forward, and climbed out to inspect. I'd bent the bumper again. I'd hit the fender again. There was a long, deep scratch in the fender of Jeff's replacement car.

Jeff accepted my news with a patient sigh. Parents!

Somebody up there is conspiring to keep us humble. God is on their side.

Coda:

Jay decreed that he would no longer make the thirty-mile trek to the airport to pick up visiting guests. The clincher was the Christmastime airport trip that took well over two hours—the trip that inspired Jay to declare that Jeff would probably be home in Chicago before we'd be back at our house in Edmonds.

We fought ice and snow, slipping and sliding, and cursed other drivers for their poor skills in navigating winter weather. We're midwesterners and accustomed to miserable driving conditions, but that trip inspired the end of our taxi service. Shuttle vans provide convenient transportation from the airport to our front door.

I am uncomfortable with this new rule. We've always been at the airport—a welcoming committee of two—with a video recorder on hand to capture the moments. Our adult children live all over the world. Their visits are special. I want to treasure every minute of their presence when they visit us.

One by one, each of our adult children has let me know that the new rule is okay with them. They're accustomed to relying on public transportation. They believe in sharing rides. In turn each one has made some small comment to me.

"Dad's driving isn't quite what it used to be," says one.

"Dad follows other cars a little too closely," opines another.

I'm puzzled. Jay has a near-perfect driving record with only a couple of tickets for minor infractions in all his years behind the wheel. We've both taken the driving course for seniors and learned to calculate the distance between our car and the one in front of us. We've promised to notify each other of any decline in the other's skills.

During the last visit from Jeff, the weather looked as if it would be unremarkable. I volunteered to drive him to the airport for his trip home. He put his hand on my shoulder.

"It's fine, Mom. The shuttle is the way to go."

In that moment, I realized that we'd come full circle. It wasn't just Jay's driving. Jay and I had once been the nervous passengers with our teenaged drivers, but the positions have switched.

Now it's the children who bite their nails and wonder if our skills are up to par.

A Working Mom

First I was a working mom. Then I became a *working* mom.

When I was a stay-at-home mother with four children, my neighbor managed to raise my (one-eighth) Irish ire by asking me to take her child to the doctor for his annual physical (she was a *working* mom who didn't have time). I had a huge daily workload with toddler ballast on every appendage, and I was being pulled in every direction. I was already the neighborhood chauffeur—the go-to mom. In my neighbor's mind, I lived a leisurely life, playing with the children and inventing things to take up my time. Neither of us fully appreciated the complexities of the other's life.

When Mark was ten years old, I rejoined the workforce. I pinned instructions above the washer and dryer and headed off to the corporate world. My work outside the home taught me a number of lessons:

1. In spite of your having juggled roles and tasks as a mother of four, prospective employers will be convinced that your mind has mildewed in your absence from the workforce.

2. Promises made by your employer—flexibility with your schedule, understanding about the demands of your family—need to be written in blood.

3. School hours are incompatible with an eight-to-five work schedule. High schools typically begin at an early hour, followed an hour later by middle school, and finally primary school. The older children who could be called upon to send the younger ones off are already at school. Schedule juggling begins. Before- and after-school care programs are a godsend. I also learned the value of a mother's time—it's a dollar a minute for every minute you delay picking up your child from these programs.

4. There are a hundred half-days in every school year. Half-days in grade school never coincide with half-days at middle or high school.

5. When you arrive home from work on most days, you will discover that one child needs a crucial supply for tomorrow's project, forcing you to go back out the door and head for the store.

6. If you have an important meeting at work, your child will become so ill that the school nurse will call and require you to leave immediately to pick him/her up because he/she is either on the verge of collapse or he/she is highly contagious and may infect the entire school. The child's father will be out of town.

7. As a corollary to number six, you will pick up your child, rush him/her to the doctor's office before he/she

collapses in front of you, and in the short distance between the school and the doctor's office, he/she will undergo a miraculous recovery.

8. Animals will also choose your work hours for sickness or worse. One late afternoon, I picked up a phone call from Annie, a college student who was providing after-school care for Mark. In a small voice, she said, "Mrs. Monroe, I think there's something wrong with the dog."

"Oh dear. Well, I'll be home in another hour."

"Mrs. Monroe, I think she's dead."

I catch my breath. "What makes you think that?"

"She's lying on the basement floor with her legs stretched out. They're stiff. And I can't see her breathing."

I do mental calculations in my head: rush-hour traffic and I was halfway across town. Jay was out of town. The vet's office would close at 5:30. "I'm on my way."

Before I left the office, I called the vet. "Please, please," I begged. "Please wait for me." Perhaps there was a chance that he could revive the dog, but if not, I could not leave a dead dog in the house all night.

I raced home and tore downstairs to examine the dog. It wasn't a difficult diagnosis—she was stiff. Annie (by choice) and Mark (by command) stayed upstairs and out of sight. I had one eye on my watch and the other on the impending vet deadline. I tried to figure out how to get this animal into the car. Finally I pushed and shoved the rigid form (no time for tears), wrapped it in an old blanket, staggered upstairs with the load clasped to my chest, and stowed it on the back seat.

I arrive at the vet's on time. No miracle awaited me there; the dog was not Lazarus. I swallowed my emotions and signed the death papers, not quite grief-stricken enough to opt for an elaborate burial in a pet cemetery, complete with an engraved headstone. I returned home to console the children.

9. Annual meetings of professional organizations always conflict with a child's important event—a championship basketball game, the state finals of a debate contest, or the scholarship recognition banquet. You will be confronted with impossible choices in which having it all is not an option.

10. There will be days when going to work will feel like you've been given permission to run away—and vice versa! You will rejoice.

RED-LETTER DAYS

An old calendar prints holidays in red. They are eye-catching reminders of special occasions and breaks from everyday routine. Staff members' vacation days are blocked in red on the office calendar. The color red prompts excitement and anticipation.

There's another side to red, though—like the red marks on exam papers highlighting our mistakes, blunders, and omissions.

There's yin and yang potential to every red-letter day. For example, two hours into cooking the Thanksgiving turkey, my oven died. A mad scramble ensued to pack up the turkey, a side dish of dressing, scalloped corn, and sweet potato casserole (all in various stages of doneness) and cart them to Mark's oven four miles away to complete the cooking process. Such an experience gives new meaning to the phrase "cold turkey."

Regardless of the outcome, red-letter days stand out.

A Romantic Vacation

"**Y**our mother deserves a vacation!" Jay declared one dinnertime.

Four heads nodded in agreement, and my spirits soared.

"I have to attend a seminar in the mountains, and you can come along. Just get somebody to stay with the kids."

The complexity of the task was overlooked with that little phrase (but that's another story). I managed to find a heaven-sent young couple who agreed to stay with our brood. Then I set about getting ready. I restocked the pantry, purchased forty meals for the freezer, took the four kids for their annual checkups to ensure that they weren't coming down with some strange malady, updated their shots, and had their teeth cleaned and hair cut. I bought them new pajamas, underwear, socks, jeans, and shirts. I cleaned the house. We updated our wills; took out another insurance policy; alerted the neighbors, grandparents, aunts, and uncles; and prepared an itinerary of our plans, complete with phone numbers and addresses. I typed out an itemized daily schedule for each child, called Sam's mother to see if she could take over the baseball car pool, checked with Jackie to see if she could take Lissy to swim lessons, and had an emergency medical release notarized at the bank.

Somehow I made it to the plane.

"I can't believe it. Nobody got sick or maimed. No emergency canceled our plans. Just think—the two of us alone!"

We held hands and settled down to enjoy the flight. I even closed my eyes for five minutes without hearing my name, "Mom."

Approximately twenty minutes into the flight, a woman across the aisle leaned over to Jay. "Are you feeling all right?"

I bolted upright. Jay was green.

"I'm fine." He smiled wanly at her.

"What's the matter?" I whispered.

"Just a touch of the flu."

I felt his head. (I am a human thermometer. My accuracy has been verified.) "You're burning up!"

He flagged down the stewardess and ordered a soda. "I'm fine." His green turned to a flushed red, and he sat doubled over. "I'll be okay." Finally he slept.

Jay was full of conversation with the driver on our trip from the airport to the mountain resort. *He's feeling better*, I told myself. When we entered our room, he collapsed.

"It's probably a twenty-four-hour bug. I'll be in perfect shape tomorrow." This was on Monday.

On Tuesday night, we chose a romantic little mountain restaurant famous for its gourmet food served in an intimate setting. The waiter seated us in a private corner. Flickering candlelight glowed in the center of a bowl of flowers.

"Order anything you want, Darling."

"What are you having?"

"I'm sorry," he confessed. "I can't eat."

"You're still sick! You haven't eaten all day?"

He nodded sheepishly. "I'm sure I'm on the mend."

I ate. He watched.

He spent that night leaning over the toilet bowl. "I'm sure I'll feel better tomorrow now that my system is cleaned out," he declared with bravado as he climbed back in bed.

On Wednesday afternoon, he took a nap. "It takes time to get adjusted to this mountain air."

We took the ski lift to the mountaintop on Thursday afternoon. The view was spectacular: a broad, expansive view of mountains and valleys, rich with summer colors. Jay turned purple. We stayed on the ski lift and made a hasty decent.

On Friday we headed home. I debated with myself on the way back. Should I call an ambulance to meet us in Denver? Jay's face was ashen.

"I can make it home," he assured me.

Four smiling faces greeted us when we arrived home. The sitters were beaming. They had survived.

"How was your trip?"

I surveyed the expectant faces. "Wonderful. Just wonderful."

Jay headed for the bedroom to call his doctor.

Father's Day,
Family-Style

Gala family celebrations are legendary in many American homes. At our house, mythical might be a better word.

I've never aspired to be this generation's Pearl Mesta—the hostess with the mostest. My ambitions are much more modest. I'd just like to throw a family celebration that didn't end in catastrophe. The saboteur takes many forms. On Father's Day, it was the chocolate cake crumb.

The celebration began well enough. I have one thing in common with Pearl: planning. The children and I decided to treat Jay to a special day at the lake. I'd heard about a new lake in an undeveloped area where fish were plentiful. We shopped for gifts, and on Saturday, nine-year-old Lissy baked a cake for Jay and five-year-old Mark helped her frost it with bright green icing.

By eleven o'clock on Sunday morning, the children had served Jay a breakfast of bacon and eggs, only slightly delayed by doughy coffee cake. The older boys were loading the dishwasher and scouring the pans. I proceeded to pack the picnic basket.

"Mom, Mom!" Lissy clamored for my attention. "Can we take the dogs?"

I made some motion of my head that she interpreted as an affirmative nod. I should have been more careful with the guest list and excluded the four-footed variety.

Jay is a gracious guest of honor. He pitched in to help. He tied the fishing poles to the luggage rack and stowed the lawn chairs, tackle boxes, and picnic basket in the trunk. Our trip was slightly complicated by the fact that Mark was recovering from surgery and wearing a body cast. We'd been housebound for weeks.

We propped Mark in the center space behind the front seat. He was flanked on either side by a dog. The three older children wound their bodies in the remaining space like pretzels, blanketed by the Sunday paper. By the time we reached the lake, the boys were self-proclaimed skeletons. Their skin was sanding their bones. We decided to eat first.

Finding a picnic area was the first hurdle. Picnic areas are more enticing from a distance. (Personally I find any wilderness more enticing from a distance.) We spotted a table surrounded by knee-high grass, which was vetoed. Danny caught a glimpse of another spot, and we hurried to claim it. On closer examination, we found that the table was situated on an island, inaccessible to humans. Now we were hanging out the car windows, peering in every direction for that elusive perfect setting. We pulled into a vacant shelter and began to unload.

"Mom!" Lissy dove back into the car. A swarm of stinging insects attacked us. The table in the knee-high grass began to look more appealing.

Lissy tied the dogs to a table leg, and we began unloading once more. Jay made a new discovery. In the depths of the plush gray carpet of the back seat, under books, comic books, and random sheets of Sunday's paper, the puppy had been sick. I discovered how difficult it is to shampoo carpeting with four-inch squares of moist towelettes.

We gathered around the table for fried chicken. Jeff brought out the pride of the younger two: the green-iced cake. Unfortunately he tripped and dropped it.

"Dogs should not be given sweets—especially sick dogs."

I had a grim expression on my face. Momentarily I forgot another rule: the hostess should always have a sense of humor.

Jay put a hand on my shoulder as we stowed the picnic remains. "It's all right. We came for the fishing, not the lunch."

The second journey around the shoreline was a search for a fishing spot. The legend on the map was clear: the two solid lines were oil roads, the dotted lines were gravel, and the two fine lines were graded roads. We chose a gravel road.

It left the main road in two narrow lanes. Over the hill, it became one lane. When we passed the pond, it deteriorated into a dirt path. We made our way over a final hump, and Jay brought the car to a jerking halt. We were confronted by an unmarked barricade, which was preceded by a mud hole. There was no lake in sight—only dense underbrush and trees.

Danny began to pester us about the time because he needed to get home to pitch a Little League game. Jeff was starving again; he was hot and his legs were cramping. Lissy hung into the front seat, chanting, "When are we gonna get there, Dad? Huh? Huh?"

I made a feeble suggestion. "If you can turn the car around, let's go to the boat ramp. At least there we can see the lake."

Jay muttered to himself as he backed up the car cautiously, jolting and jerking over the ruts. On the main road, I feigned cheerfulness. "If we hurry, we can still drop our lines in the water."

We carried the poles, chairs, and Mark and wound our way through the weeds to a sandy beach. Jay baited five hooks and wandered down shore to toss out his line. I sat in the sand, contemplating the scene before me, savoring the moment. Success! This was the real Father's Day celebration. Jay was wearing his old yellow fishing hat and faded jeans. He held his pole, mesmerized by the clear, blue, lapping water at his feet.

"Dad! Dad! My line is caught." Danny tugged and jerked at his pole. Patiently Jay propped his pole in the ground and took hold of Danny's. The line popped and we watched the bobber float away. "It's okay, Dad. I'll skip rocks instead."

The fishing passed without a bite. We headed for home as a quiet, subdued group. We hadn't caught any fish and had even lost some equipment. Defeat, I resolved, was not part of my party plan. The celebration was not beyond redemption. I turned to Jay.

"When we get home, the kids can unload the car while I fix you something cold to drink. We'll have a quiet supper on the patio."

We pulled into the driveway and got out. I reached inside for Mark and tugged at him in his body cast, inching him from the car. I stood him up and saw a chocolate cake crumb on his neck. I brushed at it. It stuck. I peered closer at the tenacious crumb. The little crumb had legs.

"Ticks!" I wilted with a sigh. "Light me a match." I disposed of the tick, and we began running fingers through our hair.

Jay was squirming. "See anything on my back?"

I was about to head for the house when I looked down at my feet. There sat puppy, wagging an innocent tail.

"Shoot!" We hadn't checked the dogs.

Jay knelt on the cement, parting the long black hair and working carefully on the pup. She had ticks in her ears, under her belly, and on her back. The car doors stood open. The vehicle was only half-unloaded. Danny shifted from one foot to the other, worrying aloud.

"Dad, Dad, I've gotta get going. The game'll start."

I sank down on the concrete. "I give up."

Jay grinned at me over the dog. "There's one thing to be said for these family hooplas. They're memorable."

A Lightning Send-off

"Some people invite catastrophe," my neighbor responded wryly, as I bemoaned my fate.

I protest. For example, the night the lightning struck. Was I outside playing Benjamin Franklin, dragging a kite across the lawn? No! I was sound asleep, oblivious to the destruction that nature was wreaking on our house.

Lightning usually strikes with violent force, producing dramatic results. Not at our house (for which I shall be eternally grateful). Midway through a raging storm, it crept in silently, stealthily, feeding along the power lines, causing the breakers to trip in our fuse box—except for one. It chose to sneak along the copper water pipe leading to the icemaker in the refrigerator. It whizzed along the copper tubing with lightning force, straight for the icemaker's motor, which it destroyed. It paused in its deadly course only long enough to burn a hole in the copper tubing behind the refrigerator. It was a tiny hole—just big enough to permit a stream of water to splay a fountain on the back of the refrigerator all night long.

When Jay and I woke the next morning—the day we were due to begin our summer vacation trip to the Rockies—we had a hurried conversation regarding our schedules before getting out of bed. Everything would have to proceed with precision if we were to leave by the planned departure time of three o'clock. I stayed in bed for another minute, planning my strategy. For that precious minute, I was organized.

I traipsed to the kitchen to get a cup of coffee and slipped in a pool of water. Bewildered, I checked under the sink and then in the little half-bath off the kitchen. Where had this deluge begun? Jay appeared in the doorway, dressed in a suit and tie, ready to hurry off to a breakfast meeting.

"A little problem?" he asked.

He eyed the scene and gingerly pulled back the refrigerator. There it was—that hole in the copper tubing, spouting its little fountain. He worked awkwardly, leaning down, trying to protect his suit from the grime on the refrigerator coils. He turned off the water supply to the icemaker and straightened.

"Honey, I'm sorry. I hate to leave you with this mess, but my meeting's at eight. Better call somebody to see what's the problem." He hesitated. "Guess we're lucky it's still under warranty."

"Bye, Dear." I eyed him from my position in the pool of water. My expression was forlorn. I fetched the mop and began sopping up water. I worked quickly, hoping to finish before the children descended to the scene.

"Mom, something's the matter up here. The hair dryer won't work."

"You'll have to wait until I'm finished here. I'll go downstairs and check the box."

Downstairs! It dawned on me. I propped the mop and hurried to the basement steps, opened the door, and peered over the railing. Sure enough our waterfall had seeped down the walls and dripped through the ceiling, leaving puddles on the floor below. I could see white splotches on a wooden tabletop. When I finished mopping upstairs, I carried my mop downstairs to repeat the process.

By nine o'clock, I had two clean floors, and the kids had fixed themselves pancakes. The kitchen was in shambles. I decided to focus on the essentials. Some things puzzled me. The dishwasher had quit midcycle the night before, and the toaster wasn't working. I put a load of dirty clothes in the washing machine and began my search for a repairman. By eleven o'clock, I actually had a man in the kitchen studying the problem. (I had pronounced it a life-and-death situation.)

"I don't know, lady. Seems like maybe your house was hit by lightning. Better call your electrician. I don't handle electrical problems. Only refrigerators." The repairman regarded my stricken face. "I won't charge for this call, warranty and all. But next time!" As he left, he added, "Might check with your insurance company."

I called the insurance agent, who was gracious. "Just let me know what the bill is. We'll cover everything over the deductible." I felt comforted.

Electricians are elusive people, but I was determined. I begged. The electrician's answering service gave me a home phone number. I called and found out from his wife that he was working on a site a few miles away. "Look for a white pickup and ask for Joe."

I left explicit instructions with the four kids. "Fold the clothes when they're done drying and pack your bags. We need to be ready to leave when I get home."

I set out on my mission, stalking my prey. I found the subdivision and spotted a white truck. I pulled in behind it and got out, tottering over wooden boards placed on a muddy path that led to a half-open frame structure. Two workmen stared at me.

"Is one of you Joe?" They shook their heads. "I'm looking for Joe, the electrician."

One shrugged. "Might try that house at the end of the next street."

I cruised the streets, searching. No white pickup. Finally I spotted a white vehicle. Someone was sitting in it. I pulled up beside it and hollered at the man. "Joe?"

He shook his head. My heart sank as I exhaled. I was about to leave when he pointed toward a house. "Joe's working in there. He'll be out shortly."

I parked, blocking the truck's path. I listened to the radio and drummed my fingers on the dashboard, waiting for Joe. The man had no idea of the value of my time. He finished his work and stood in the doorway conversing with his client for ten minutes. It was nearly two o'clock. Finally he headed for his truck and I jumped out of my car.

"Joe, I'm desperate!"

He stopped short, gaping at me with an odd expression on his face.

"I've got to have you check our electrical system before we leave on vacation in another hour. The refrigerator man thinks lightning struck our power lines, and we have no power in half of our outlets. There's water in the electrical box." I knew I was babbling. I paused for breath and begged. "Please follow me to my house and check it out."

Desperation carried the hour. Not only did Joe come to the house—he sopped up the water, checked the outlets, dried out the breakers, and ordered a new breaker to replace the one that had been destroyed. My dishwasher worked again. The hair dryer was back on duty. The toaster functioned. We could leave.

Jay made one last trip to the house. "Think I'll turn off the water supply to the house, just in case."

When we returned from vacation, we had the motor on the icemaker replaced and the electrical box fixed. I totaled up the bills: $499.75. We had a $500 deductible on our insurance policy.

A Wet Blanket

I didn't plan to evolve into a wet blanket—it just happened. Without a doubt, it is related to some trauma in childhood. As I was one of six children, I place disproportionate value on the term *private bath.*

When spring arrives in our part of the country, not only do flowers appear—vehicles do as well. The highways are dotted with campers and RVs. It begins as a trickle, but by midsummer, it develops into a flood. They're everywhere. This points to a mania sweeping the country: Americans—accustomed to traveling with everything but the kitchen sink—now take the kitchen sink.

There seems to be something unpatriotic about having an aversion to camping. "Where's your pioneering spirit?" my husband asks.

"About two centuries behind," I respond. "Would you be thrilled if it suddenly became possible for you to take the office with you on a wilderness vacation, in an abbreviated and rustic form—like a typewriter instead of a laptop?"

I must admit, I have fallen prey to the glories extolled at camper shows. Spacious, clean, brightly colored campers beckon me to share the great outdoors. (Sometimes I forget that even an empty closet can look commodious.) The salesman boasted about the utilitarian approach: a place for everything, and every inch of space is functional. As I soon discovered, there are no empty corners. (On my list of desired household attributes after *private bath* is *empty corners*.)

My husband, our four children, and I began our camping adventures with a foldout trailer. It was a small, neat box that trailed inconspicuously behind the car. Upon arrival at the campsite, it revealed itself to be a desert ship. The ends rolled out, the sides rolled up, the counters folded in, the curtains hung down, the steps pulled out, and all of it took place in sequential order. (I should have considered it an omen about camping when our youngest child proceeded to vomit upon completion of our first setup.)

One Saturday in the middle of March, we pulled our brand new camper away from the sales office and immediately made plans to try it out the next weekend at a nearby state park. We left home on a promising sunny afternoon, drove fifty miles into clouds and rain, and spent the entire weekend in a drizzle. This camper did not lack a mudroom; it *became* a mudroom. The weather did not dampen our enthusiasm—just our jeans, shoes, sheets, matches, and playing cards.

The second weekend excursion was spent in a camping area in a neighboring city. We visited relatives and declined all invitations to stay with them.

"We have the camper," we demurred and drove back to it in the evening. A spring chill had invaded the air, but we were undaunted. Our camper had a space heater. In the morning, our pillows were frozen to the walls of the camper and morning dew covered the blankets. Togetherness was a necessity as we clung to each other, trying to get warm. The blower on our heater rattled noisily, heating a two-foot space in front of it. It was like heating a kitchen with a candle.

These trips were mere trial runs. We mapped out a cross-country jaunt—one of those "last big trip while all the kids can go" vacations. The camper seemed like an economical solution to traveling with four children. We disregarded the initial investment because—as everyone knows—"You can always get your money back when you sell the camper."

Preparation for the trip included assigning numbered tasks to each person. Twenty nights of putting up the camper required a system, so we practiced. I stationed myself with a clipboard, checking off assignments as they were completed.

"Danny, you're responsible for number five. Hand your dad that crank. Lissy, be prepared for eight and twelve." We timed ourselves.

On the battlefield, it's always different. At midnight, we found the child for tasks six and ten asleep, so in hushed voices new tasks were added. "Somebody take Mark to the bathroom." "Hold that flashlight still—I can't see the level."

One night, finding the campground after midnight, we managed to set the camper up with a twist in its frame. All night long, every time Danny breathed, the camper squeaked.

"Dammit, don't breathe!" was an exasperated four-in-the-morning command. The cause of the trouble was not evident until daylight.

If a camper is merely a traveling bed or a place to eat, it offers convenience. If the weather turns sour and the camper is living space, it strains the nerves.

"Get lost!" can only mean a drop-off at the next gas station—there is no such thing as *get lost* in a camper. You bump elbows when reading. You can only get into the ice chest if your posterior is in the doorway. I discovered that I could make coffee by leaning out of bed, although we had to get up to drink it—the bed was the table (upside down).

After our long trip was over, we decided to sell the camper. I confessed that for *my* vacation, I wanted to be pampered. I wanted to soak in a hot tub and spend an hour dressing. I wanted to sink into a rocker after a long day's drive and banish the kids to some other building. I liked my togetherness in smaller doses.

Lissy and Mark had an organized patter that began: "Hey, see that neat camper we passed, Mom? Now there's one you'd really like. Roomy, too!"

I took my stand. I was firm in my position.

The weather turned warm again. A southerly wind blew breezes of gulf air through our plains state, and Jay pulled a thick brochure from his briefcase while we were reading the evening newspaper.

"This fellow at the office has a fifth wheel."

"A what?"

"A fifth wheel. It pulls behind a pickup. Now that's traveling! Remember those mornings we got up at dawn and I fixed sausage, eggs, and pancakes on the picnic table? You said food had never tasted better."

A pleasant memory teased my mind. I stiffened my resistance.

"*Any* food someone else prepares has a special flavor. In my view, camping is just a phase in family life and I'm beyond that phase." I turned the page of the newspaper. "If you're going to pull a house-sized trailer, you might as well own a cabin."

Jay's eyes narrowed slightly. "Somebody called me about one down on the river—just a simple fishing cabin . . . "

Uninvited Guest

For a number of years, my entertaining was largely confined to supervising hordes of wild children at sleepovers and birthday parties. My attempts at formal entertaining were rare, but occasionally, I tried.

One of Jay's employees was the proud father of a new baby boy. John and his wife, Lee, had waited a number of years to start their family, and John's delight at his new son was contagious. I invited them to our house for dinner to celebrate.

These two professionals had morphed into hypervigilant parents. Even though the baby was now several weeks old, they would not leave this precious child with anyone. They did not take him out in public where he could come in contact with *germs.* After some coaxing, they accepted our invitation with the proviso that they bring the baby with them. Since we were old hands at parenting, we assured them that the baby would be fine. Our children were banished to the lower level of the house for the evening with strict instructions to be quiet and invisible, and to refrain from maiming a sibling. The adults' dinner would be served with china and crystal; the kids ate a picnic supper on paper plates in the family room.

The baby was beautiful, and I was allowed to hold him for a moment. We spent the first hour of the evening oohing and ahhing over the baby until he fell asleep. Lee and I put him in the middle of our king-sized bed and fenced him in with varying sizes of pillows and rolled-up quilts (no soft blankets to potentially smother him) just in case this extraordinary baby was an athletic little being who might roll and flip off the bed. We left him safely ensconced on his throne and returned to dinner in the dining room. I served the salad, hot bread, and entrée. We sat at the table for a long time, lingering over adult conversation. Finally I stirred myself and got up to clear the dishes, refusing offers of help from Lee.

"You're a new mother. You deserve a rest. Just relax."

I carried the dirty dishes to the kitchen and pulled the door shut behind me to preserve the quiet for our guests. I heaped the dishes on the counter for later tackling, then cut slices of cherry cheesecake. I placed them on delicate antique china plates and opened the drawer to pull out dessert forks. Swooosh! A small, gray mouse jumped out of the drawer and leapt to the floor. I stifled a scream, and in my moment of horror, I realized that the little demon had disappeared. I stood, shell-shocked. I pictured our guests grabbing up their sleeping child, fleeing from this pestilence.

I gathered myself together, ran to the linen closet for a clean towel, and soaped and dried the dessert forks, keeping an eye out for the malevolent intruder. Before reentering the dining room, I pasted on my best smile. I served our guests, poured tiny cups of rich, dark coffee, and stewed. The kitchen door was firmly shut, but would the critter escape?

The relaxed conversation continued for another hour as we left the table and retired to the living room. I was on high alert. My mind raced through scenarios as I forced myself to participate in the easy patter that takes place after a leisurely meal. I tried to keep my eyes from darting around the room, seeking any sign of the uninvited guest.

Finally Lee stood up and stifled a yawn. "Time to go. Sorry, it's those nighttime feedings." She smiled. "Let me get the bottle from your refrigerator."

"I'll get it." I raced to the kitchen door.

They bundled up the baby and said their good-byes. The car lights were at the end of the drive when I gasped at Jay.

"There's a mouse in the house."

I tore out to the kitchen. At midnight I was transformed into a scullery maid. I pulled out every drawer, washed every dish, and threw all the kitchen linens into the washing machine while Jay scoured the house looking for the little gatecrasher—to no avail. He had vanished. I scarcely closed my eyes that night as I plotted revenge. Visions of big steel traps baited with mountains of cheese filled my mind.

The next morning, we found a small hole in the house, left by the builder on the north brick wall. This was the probable entrance. We set traps without success. A few days later, the children and I spotted the creature as it scurried downstairs to the lower level. We chased it with brooms, and, cornering it, whacked at it until it collapsed. Jay says it died of a heart attack or combat fatigue. I prefer to think of it as succumbing to the peril of being an uninvited guest.

A Motel Like No Other

"Make your reservations at the Splendid Ten Motel. I've put a hold on twenty rooms," Cindy (the niece in charge of our family reunion) advised.

Jay called to make reservations for our adult children and us. The price was comparable to that of a major metropolitan area, which was surprising, since the motel was in a town of 1,600 people.

"It's not on the interstate. I wonder why the price is so high?" I asked.

"Could be a monopoly, like that old dinner choice: take it or leave it."

We drove through rolling midwestern farm country where the stalks of corn were green and six feet tall. The darker green soybeans stretched out in neat rows across the fields. Pheasants and red-winged blackbirds flew in front of our car. We passed a badger squashed by a previous motorist. At least it wasn't a skunk, I thought.

The Splendid Ten Motel was a large, boxy, two-story structure of red brick and sandstone, devoid of any redeeming architectural features. Its front entrance led to a hall dividing the lobby on one side from a small breakfast area on the other. A prominent sign proclaimed "No Dogs Allowed."

Our first-floor room numbers were in a series of three hundred. The motel employed a unique numbering system: 100s were the right wing, 200s were on the left, and straight ahead, toward the back, were the 300-series rooms. Numbers flowed around the hall—302 was across from 322. It reminded me of the adage: Think outside the box.

The complimentary breakfast sounded promising; perhaps that accounted for the price. This was farm country, the land of plenty. I envisioned fresh fruit, waffles, eggs, sausage, bacon, homemade biscuits, and kolaches (buttery pastries filled with fruit preserves).

Our breakfast the first morning consisted of watery coffee; sugary juice of undetermined origin; packaged, dry cake doughnuts; and cheap white bread that you could toast—or not. We patronized the local eatery instead.

A dusky rose carpet covered the floor of our room—or was it simply a dirty pink? Dim lighting prevented us from determining which was correct. Two queen-sized beds, a low-slung dresser, a table, and a straight-backed chair completed the furnishings, and there was a bathroom in one corner. The sink was tucked into the entryway—with a counter space of three inches on each side. A small plastic coffee maker brewed one cup at a time.

"Place the Styrofoam cup beneath the drip spout." We went without coffee.

My pillow was a solid lump of polyester. It could have begun its life in a traditional pillow shape, but repeated use and washings resulted in a square that I could not punch, pull, twist, or stretch into anything other than a dense, unyielding mass. My neck stiffened more with each passing night. I developed cavewoman slouch.

However, it was the two framed prints hanging above the bed that set the motel room apart from all others. As I faced the bed each evening, ready to begin my tussle with the pillow, I gazed at these pictures. A dappled springer spaniel stared at me with doleful eyes, his jaws clenching a flaccid pheasant. No bloodied body parts were visible. The pheasant, with an invisible mortal wound, appeared to be at peace. The companion portrait was of a golden retriever, posing with the placid look of a job well done. His mouth clamped around a dead, limpid, teal-colored duck. The bird had a faint smile upon its beak.

What demented mind chose these paintings to adorn the wall? Was there a message? Was this preparation for eternal rest? What was hiding behind the shower curtain?

In the Splendid Ten Motel, mine was a tortured sleep.

ANIMAL,
VEGETABLE . . .

When I imagine St. Francis of Assisi, I picture him in an Eden-like garden, surrounded by animals, his love suffusing all. We lesser mortals do not easily replicate this.

As a farm child, I thought chickens were dirty, snakes were frightening, and worms—sneaked into my pocket by my brother—were cause for screams and tattling. As an adult, I'm a fair-weather birder, shivering in my van while heartier souls trudge through rain and fields of mud to get a glimpse of an eagle family.

Doghouse, No Dog

Our latest home purchase came with a large doghouse in a fenced part of the backyard. Jay saw the doghouse as an opportunity or an invitation. He had his feelers out.

When it comes to pets, a birdcage gets my vote. As a mother of young children, I resisted any and all contact with the animal world vigorously—but not successfully. My stance was a solitary one. My children and a host of others wheedled and cajoled me into becoming a pet owner. The children began pestering me with, "But why did *you* get to have a goat when you were little, Mom?" and ended with something about a pet teaching them responsibility.

Whenever I think of mothers and pets, I remember my Aunt Gretchen leaning over Mother's buffet, teaspoon in hand, gingerly trying to rescue twenty guppies my cousin had dumped into a drawer of white table linens.

In spite of my foot-dragging, we had our share of pets. Our dentist had a tank full of exotic fish. They seemed like ideal pets. Their presence provided an air of tranquility (our house definitely needed tranquility). One afternoon the children and I wandered through the pet section of a local superstore. A beaming clerk pursued us.

"Today we're giving a free goldfish to every child."

The children were delighted. I surrendered an additional ten dollars for a bowl, water conditioner, rocks, ferns, and food. The fish were installed on an end table in our living room. Those finned fellows survived numerous accidents. One lost a tail at the hands of a small boy who knocked the fish bowl onto the carpet and tried to grab its flopping body. As the weeks passed, the children's interest waned, and I found myself changing the water, cleaning the bowl, and reminding people to feed them.

One evening as Jay and I were reading the paper, I said, "I'm sick and tired of caring for those aquatic acrobats and their slimy bowl."

The next morning, there they were . . . belly-up. In a flood of guilt, I sent their remains to sewer heaven. Do unloved goldfish commit suicide?

The loss of the goldfish was not a catastrophe. I can't say the same for losing the turtles. We had several turtles before I read the horror stories about turtle diseases. We had no knack for keeping them alive. There were tears when the first turtle died, and the boys had a funeral in the backyard with neighborhood children in attendance. I replaced that turtle with another. The ceremony lessened with each succeeding demise.

I sought Jay's attention one evening. "Another turtle has expired."

He wrapped it in toilet paper and stuck it in the garbage can.

The best pet we ever had was a birdcage—a leftover from a rented house. I recognized its value when my four-year-old nephew spent an entire afternoon sitting on our sidewalk trying to catch a bird to fill the cage. In ensuing years, many children spent hours trying to catch a bird.

Their dream bird was the perfect pet. It talked, sang, and performed tricks on command. Its idyllic image was protected when I refused the offer of a free bird. A bird on the wing is definitely worth two in the cage.

I'd rank gerbils close behind a birdcage as the most desirable pet. We babysat a gerbil for three weeks. Ray was delivered in a glass aquarium covered with a wire top. The tank was filled with shredded paper. Our neighbor explained, "Ray is in there. Just put water-soaked bread in the cage—that's all you have to do."

Since I am not fond of rodents, I was not thrilled to be living with this one. We shared a mutual contempt. In the weeks that Ray lived with us, I never saw him. The bread disappeared, and no strange odors emitted from the cage. We returned the aquarium and were assured that Ray had survived.

No family is complete without a dog. I've heard the same opinion about cats, but we were spared. Danny was allergic to cats. Sherry (a Manchester Chihuahua) was a Christmas present from Grandma—my mother. She had secured prior permission from me. (I had suffered from a temporary lapse in judgment.) Three-year-olds and five-year-olds don't train dogs—mothers do. The dog added a whole new dimension to my schedule.

The first year of Sherry's life with us was an iffy one. "If that dog chews on the couch again . . . if that dog doesn't shut up . . ."

We advertised Sherry for sale, and then I cried when someone inquired about buying her. Somehow Sherry made it through her first year with us and survived another thirteen. Sherry was followed by a mutt, a poodle, and two Shih Tzus.

Now that we're dogless once again, Jay is eyeing the vacant kennel.

"Our neighbor will give us one of his Lab pups," he announces.

In my book, it's a toss-up for the *perfect* pet: a birdcage or an empty doghouse.

The Purple Martin Birdhouse

A friend of mine once bid on a house simply because its owners left their organ behind. As a musician, she wanted that organ; the house was secondary. I could laugh at her, but then again, one of the reasons we bought a house was the purple martin birdhouse.

We were attracted to the house by its location on a Mississippi bayou. However, the house became even more desirable when we were greeted by dozens of purple martins swooping in and out of an elegant, octagonal, bird condominium perched in the yard. This four-story, white, wooden structure with a sea-green roof appeared to be the most desirable bird property on the waterfront. It had twenty-four units, each with its own portal and rail.

Purple martins are admirable birds with monogamous, gregarious natures. These sociable creatures perform the Herculean task of eating masses of flying insects for a homeowner.

When we got down to finalizing our purchase of the house, we hit a sticking point. Take the appliances, the owners said. Ask for anything you like—*except* the birdhouse. The birdhouse was off limits and non-negotiable!

The birdhouse and its twenty-foot pole had been a gift. It was not for sale.

We capitulated. After all, we could buy another bird-house. They weren't moving the birds—or so we thought.

Once the trauma of our move was over and the birds had left for the winter, we bought ourselves a housewarming gift: a purple martin birdhouse kit. In the catalog picture, it resembled the one the previous owners took with them—an octagonal, four-story structure. It looked easy to assemble. We bought a ground pole and accompanying telescoping pole, along with a book about purple martins.

The birdhouse package arrived and it was stunningly small. It was no more than four inches deep and about twelve inches square. We were puzzled. Had we received only a partial shipment? Jay slit the seams of the package to examine its contents. The siding was piled in neat little stacks. Each piece had predrilled holes for assembly with tiny bolts. Adjoining strips, packages of rails, and many sacks of bolts, washers, and nuts spilled out. Beneath the pieces of flooring was a huge piece of paper, folded and refolded so that it fit into the box—the directions. I have come to discover that assembly time corresponds to the size of the paper the instructions are printed on. These instructions covered the tabletop.

Our first task was sorting. Each size and shape went into its own little pile. Jay stashed the directions at our feet to free up the table for the multitude of stacks. Finally we were ready for assembly. The only easy job proved to be putting together the flooring. Pieces of siding had to be held at precisely the right angle and bolted together, using joint strips to create the octagonal building shape. I tried holding the little siding pieces at this odd angle while Jay bolted them together. Not only were the bolts small—there were different sizes for different jobs. We soon discovered that adult fingers are not the ideal size for gripping small bolts. Tiny washers and nuts spewed from our fingertips as if they'd been greased. The project began to resemble a late-night Christmas Eve session with "easy-to-assemble" toys. Indeed, elfin engineers had designed this kit for pygmy carpenters.

The assembly and attachment of the roof was equally frustrating. Eight hours after we began, the last little white plastic rail was fitted into its holes. We are eternal optimists who always think the next task will be easier. Surely there was nothing to cementing in the ground pole, fitting the birdhouse on top of the telescoping pole, and slipping it into place. Actually we discovered that it takes the skill of a circus acrobat to balance a fifteen-foot pole topped by a birdhouse while easing it into the ground pole.

Eventually, however, the birdhouse was installed high above the bayou. We only had to await early spring, when adult birds would fly in to scope out the new rentals. All spring I kept an eye peeled for our first arrival. I squealed in delight when a bird flew near the house. When summer arrived and the birdhouse still sat empty, I gave up.

"Next year!"

After the third year, we moved the birdhouse to a more open area. When we sold the house, we did not list the purple martin birdhouse as an exclusion.

"Take it!" I wanted to shout. "Experience your own empty nest syndrome."

Yard Fight: Woman versus Squirrel

The window above my computer was open. I kept typing, alert for a specific sound—a quick scramble up the trellis and a *scrush* sound announcing the assault.

I was ready when it came and roared through the house to the patio door. I grabbed a waiting weapon—a broom—and charged.

I sped after my foe, who scurried down vines, propelling himself forward and leaping over steps. He escaped into the cedar tree.

This criminal squirrel was stealing sweet water from my hummingbird feeder. Nothing seemed to deter him—not hanging the feeder on a stiff wire far from the scaffolding of the trellis, or placing a plastic umbrella over it, or lowering the feeder two feet where it would be out of reach, or taping over the feeder holes closest to the trellis. After each failed new strategy, I found squirrel traces on the red lid covering the feeder. There was no need for DNA—he left his muddy paw prints on its surface.

I bought a shepherd's crook from which to hang the feeder and placed it in a half-barrel filled with pink and red penstemons, which sat beside the trellis. I eyed the trellis from my desk chair, hoping to catch a glimpse of the squirrel's crushed demeanor when he found the feeder out of reach.

Instead, the squirrel clambered up the wooden frame. His small, furry face peeked out from fall-colored vines. He scrambled onto the empty wire hanger, his claws frantically encircling the thick, metal thread. He balanced. I held my breath. In one daring movement, he let go, plopping onto the red plastic cover of the feeder below. He looked surprised. His feet slid wildly as he drank.

I yelled and pounded the windowpane with my fist. The squirrel somersaulted off the feeder, dropping into the green stalks of the flowers below, and scampered off. Moments later I saw him peeking tentatively over the edge of the barrel, seeking a path to the black iron crook. He attempted an approach from several angles, and then departed. I pulled the barrel four feet away from the trellis, inviting no more acrobatic feats.

Shortly after dawn one morning, the squirrel poised himself on the trellis, completing his morning ablutions. He scratched his hip, rubbed his paws together, and picked at his furry coat. He turned his rodent face toward me. He moved about, searching for the feeder below, and saw only empty space. Puzzled, he inched one way, then another. Finally he spotted the red feeder suspended in the container, far from the trellis. The squirrel was transfixed. Then, without warning, he launched himself, flying toward the feeder. His body splayed wildly in the space between trellis and treat. He landed with a thud, the feeder swaying in huge arcs as he scrambled to hold on. He lapped at the sweet water splashing through the tiny holes, then lost his grip and plunged into the greenery below, mashing the stems. I rapped on the glass and hurried outside. He fled the scene. I dragged the barrel farther away.

Our morning paper featured an article on squirrels. It appeared that squirrel had become the new meat *du jour* in Britain. It posed a whole new solution to my pesky problem.

Did I have it in me to sentence him to the chopping block?

One Hot Tomato

I became a gardener late in life—after forty. I should have had a genetic predisposition since my father was a farmer, but early in life, I showed little promise.

The summer Dad was recovering from surgery, my sister and I were given the task of weeding his garden. We were not enthusiastic. In fact we were downright annoyed. We had four brothers, but somehow they escaped the assignment. Once engaged, Sis and I attacked those nasty weeds with vigor. We began with the rows of peas. We wielded our hoes like pickaxes, chopping at each little green invader, making sure we had excised it down to the lowest level of root. We were proud of our work and, as soon as Dad could venture outside, we led him (limping after us) to the garden. We looked forward to this inspection. We knew he would be happy with our efforts. He reached the rows of peas and stopped, mouth agape.

"What happened to the melons?"

"Huh?" My sister and I eyed each other.

My dad sighed and made a motion with his hands—large, roughened hands that he gestured with when he talked.

"The melons are always planted with the peas. When one crop is done, the other takes over." He shook his head. "You mean to tell me you don't know a melon plant?"

He slumped back to the house with his head drooping.

Later when he recounted this to Mother—a tone of incredulity still coloring his words—I offered my opinion.

"You have to admit we were pretty thorough." Only one small melon plant had survived our machetes.

My gardening since then has retained some characteristics of that early venture—education by error.

As a child, I ate bushels of huge, red, luscious, juicy tomatoes grown by my father under a hot, midwestern sun. Now, living in the Northwest, the tomatoes I buy have no taste and no juice. Eating one is like biting into a tennis ball. Thus I decided that I would grow tomatoes. Surely I could produce tomatoes as tasty as my father's. The gardening section of our newspaper listed varieties of tomatoes that flourished in our region. I began making a shopping list.

In late February, I was shopping at a local nursery. I spotted an employee with the words "Master Gardener" embroidered on his shirt. I sidled up to him, peppering him with questions about how to best tackle the task of growing good tomatoes. He stopped working and leaned on a shovel handle.

"Let me tell you about my tomatoes. I had my best-ever crop last year." His mouth worked as he recalled the taste.

"How did you do it?"

"You have to make up for our cool summers, give 'em heat. Plant your tomatoes next to a south wall, cut up strips of red plastic—the kind your newspapers come in—and put them around the base of the plant. Next there is the

Wall of Water. You really get a head start by surrounding your plants with warm water."

I dug in my purse, searching for a pen. I found one, but not a scrap of paper.

"Wait a minute," I begged. "What is this Wall of Water thing, and do you have any?"

He pointed at a shelf. I grabbed the product he had indicated and began writing notes on the plastic package.

He regaled me with tales of his tomatoes. One of his tomato plants had out-produced nine of his neighbor's.

I left the store laden with soil amendments, wire mesh cages, one-inch plastic plumbers' pipe, and—of course—the Wall of Water in its plastic package (with my handwritten notes).

In May I bought tomato plants. Jay helped me (with the promise of a truly good tomato as a reward). He built a six-by-eight-foot pen at the south corner of our house. We poured sacks of soil, manure, sand, and other amendments into the pen. A veritable banquet awaited those tomato plants. I gently tucked the fledgling tomatoes into the soil. We dug in plumbing pipe to feed the developing roots. I surrounded the plants with the Wall of Water; it was like amniotic fluid for the elfin beauties.

The little green plants remained small. Weeks passed with the tomatoes tucked inside the water-laden plastic walls. I groused and grumbled like a worried mother. One of the plants was supposed to deliver ripe tomatoes in sixty days, but I soon realized that it would take steroids to accomplish that feat.

By the first of July, it was apparent the magic wasn't working. Although the plants were beginning to overflow the plastic walls, there were few blossoms. The four tomato plants Jay had set in plain ground a few feet away were developing small, green gumballs of fruit.

By mid-August, Jay's plants had loads of green-and-red tomatoes. My planned beauties failed to meet any expectations. Where had I gone wrong? Was it too much food? Too little water? Had I used the right kind of manure? Where was my one hot tomato?

Meanwhile in my front garden, a large bouquet bloomed. Rich, dark green leaves hugged the earth beneath stalks of sweet-smelling royal purple—the velvety blossoms of a heliotrope. I hadn't planted it. Had it been placed by birds or a squirrel?

Gardening teaches us larger life lessons. Even with the best-laid plans, the end results are out of our control, and life provides unexpected gifts.

MOVING ON

Our lives progress with a fluidity that leaves us bewildered, wondering how we got from there to here. It happens so quickly. Along the way, we change houses, we remodel and redecorate, and we end old projects and begin new ones.

The children grow up and out—from babies to college students and beyond. The accordion years—the years when they leave home, only to move back in—end with the off-spring all on their own.

Throughout there's a constant: me. Some days I ride my bike and momentarily feel the urge to fling my arms and legs wide, and fly along with the wild abandon of a ten-year-old. Could I still do it? Do I dare to try? I'm the same person on the seat—just older.

It Was a
Moving Experience

I sat looking at piles of vanilla packing-paper and yellow boxes ready to be filled with the detritus of forty-plus years of married life. For a few minutes, I paused, remembering all the other moves that have punctuated our married life.

Recently I met a rarity—a man who had never moved. Personally I'm cousin to the nomads of the camel trains. For our family, moving was added to life's inevitable duo: death and taxes. Packing boxes delineated various stages in our life cycle. Jay and I moved eleven times in the first seventeen years of our marriage and have moved several times since. We learned from it all, but there's a price to pay for all this education.

Our first move was a snap. We gave notice and moved from a second-floor walkup to a basement walkdown. We carried clothes, dishes, and a few miscellaneous items down a fire escape, loaded them into our compact car, and hauled them five blocks to another furnished apartment. It was our only simple move.

By the time our first child arrived, we were back on a second floor. We acquired a whole new set of possessions with the baby, including a bassinet, crib, walker, stroller, high chair, sterilizer, bottle-warmer, and—of course—dirty clothes.

I begrudged the Laundromat every dollar it swallowed and decided we needed a washing machine. Jay and two friends removed the stair rail and lugged our new machine up the narrow staircase to our apartment. Two months later, they did it again for our next move—two hundred miles away, where Jay had gotten a new job.

An appraisal of our belongings led us to conclude that a compact car was no longer an adequate moving vehicle. We borrowed a pickup truck. Baby made the trip by car. His seat was wedged between boxes and bedding, with a vining philodendron draped over the top.

The scale of moving runs from do-it-yourself to leave-it-to-them. The turning point is inevitably a monumental, Herculean effort. If you survive it, you vow never to do it again. Our last and biggest do-it-yourself move was made with Jay driving a rental truck five hundred miles to our new home. Three-year-old Jeff was a willing copilot for his dad. I drove our car and trailed behind the truck with Danny (our one-and-a half-year-old) as my passenger. Normally I considered myself an attentive mother, but for this trip, following the truck was my obsession. Sounds issuing from the back seat elicited the same response from me for five hundred miles—corn curls, crackers, cookies, and crunchies handed over the back of the seat.

We arrived in our new city to find the temperature a record-breaking 107 degrees. We had planned to unload the truck ourselves, but Jay checked with a local labor pool and found someone to help (for an hourly fee). This young man was an avid devotee of the midwestern work ethic and believed in giving extra value for every dollar earned.

By midafternoon, Jay tugged at his shirt (which was plastered to his back with perspiration) and suggested the two of them take a break. The young man responded with a haughty look, consigning Jay to the ranks of the decrepit.

"Go right ahead, Mister. I'll just keep on working."

Jay was not to be outdone, but that kid nearly worked him to death.

Thus we joined the throngs who leave it to the professionals. We hired our first moving company when we bought a house from a couple called the Stocktons, who were moving a thousand miles away. They were to be out on Monday—we were to move in on Wednesday—and new residents would occupy our vacant house on Thursday.

On Monday night, Jay got a call. There had been a mix-up, and the Stocktons' movers had not shown up. Could we possibly delay our move a day or two? That was when we discovered—as if on some huge game board—that all moves in America, on any given day, are linked in a gigantic chain. Delays are impossible. Thus it was on Wednesday afternoon (as we were moving *into* the house) that the Stocktons were moving *out*. To make room for us, the Stocktons' movers carried all their possessions to the front lawn first, then to the truck afterward.

Five moving men, a cleaning woman, and four harried householders were tested beyond endurance, culminating in the Stocktons' moving men getting an old upright piano stuck in the hallway that led to the only bathroom, bedrooms, and basement. This was a puzzle demanding the input of every man in the house. They wiggled, twisted, inched, and turned that piano. They removed all the doors leading into the hall. After half an hour of maneuvering the up-ended instrument, they finally cleared the hall. The flow of yellow boxes in-and-out and up-and-down resumed. That night I closed the curtains on the scene outside: the Stocktons' movers patiently loading their truck from the assemblage on the front lawn.

The point at which a family hires professional movers often coincides with becoming homeowners. Now part of moving consists of "showing the house" (which compares to a torture rack). For days and weeks prior to moving, I have jumped out of bed at an ungodly hour to attack my work: make the beds, scour the bathrooms, swoop the dishes out from under the dawdlers at the table, and police the walls with a damp cloth. Showers are permitted only between midnight and six o'clock in the morning. It is no longer possible to throw a few things out of sight in a closet. *They* (the potential buyers) look in closets.

One realtor provided me with a brochure giving advice on how to prepare our house for sale. It suggested that I clean out the closets, leave the lights on, have a sparkle in the bathrooms, and have good smells emanating from the kitchen. I tried. I trained the children and their friends to leave their shoes in the entryway, suggesting that we were hosting a marathon old-fashioned sock hop. My oven was clean—a rarity—and I vowed that food prepared by my hand would never again be baked in its racks.

Good smells were my stumbling block. If we were ever to contract bubonic plague, it would probably be on a moving day. While some people declare that moving is enough to make them sick, with us it's literal—not just heartsick, but real, old-fashioned, physically deep-down sick—the kind of sickness you can't fake.

When Lissy was three, a half hour after the packers arrived, she pattered out to the kitchen in her pink flannel nightgown.

"What is this on my neck, Mommy?"

I took one look and ran downstairs. As a matter of courtesy, I inquired, "Are you men afraid to stay in the house? My daughter seems to have contracted chicken pox."

The younger of the two—a muscular, redheaded, six-footer—flashed me a horrified expression. "You'll have to call the company, lady. I've never had 'em." Then he beat it for the door. Chicken pox cancelled babysitting arrangements, too.

Another move was sabotaged by the flu. The realtor notified me that our house would be the focus of a grand tour on Monday morning. Every realtor from his firm would march through the premises to become acquainted with the features of our abode. At six o'clock on Monday morning, Mark awakened me with a gurgling sound. I was too late. He had vomited on the sheets, blanket, bedspread, and floor. As I was loading the washer, I kept thinking about the requirement for homey smells. This didn't seem to fit.

Mark's flu lasted for days. I sprayed scent, lit candles, turned on fans, and opened windows. I washed his bedding fourteen times and took long drives with him and the dog (to keep us company). Sure enough, the dog caught Mark's flu.

The climax occurred on an evening when the realtor called. He had a family who wanted to make an offer on the house. How soon could they come over?

By then Jay had relocated to his new job, so I was left to load four children, the dog, and emergency carsick bags into the car and cruise. For two hours we drove past the house, around the block, to the drive-in window of a restaurant for coffee and soda, and past the house again. We survived, and the house was sold.

Somehow we have survived all of our moves. Moving days are D-days in the life of a family. They are markers—points in your history. You remember them. For each one of them, I can give you concise, detailed weather data. On the December day that we moved into the house on Forty-Seventh Street, it rained, changed to sleet by midday, and finished up with snow.

Moving carries a whole range of experiences with it, but it is similar to death in an emotional sense. There is a period of mourning for friends and friendships left behind. There is a longing for the familiar—the return of the comfortable routine of daily life. Little things become monumental. I have found myself craving curtains that fit and shades that pull. However, along with that trauma comes opportunity. It provides a chance to change—not only your home, but also your life. (It is also one of the few acceptable excuses for resigning as Cub Scout den mother.)

Moving provides the impetus for us to renew and strengthen ties. In a new setting, we are all shipmates. We inhabit a lonely island in a strange sea. I attended an open-house school night only two weeks after we had arrived in a new city. As the mother of four school-aged children, I had known everyone in my children's old school—teachers and parents. At the new school, I looked around and didn't know a soul. I was completely on my own.

I knew that looming ahead of us was an orderly, comfortable life, one just as happy as the one we left behind. I also knew I'd need courage, stamina, and a willingness to wait it out until we got there. Its approach was always signaled when the garbage collectors finally put us on their list and Lissy entered the house, pulling a dark-haired girl of the same height, announcing, "This is Carrie—my new friend."

Back to the packing! Just like that day long ago, I find myself looking forward to a comfortable, new life—where, like Lissy, I can come to know "my new friend."

The Remodel

Last fall we decided to downsize, like millions of our contemporaries. For this latest move, there was no child to get the flu and no dog to evict. Jay was working out of town. I lived a Spartan life, jumping out of bed every morning to dust, vacuum, wax, and spray. I cooked nothing. The house sold, and then the trials began.

We vowed to purchase another house only after ours was sold. This put quite a limited timeframe on our finding a new house. We played with the idea of moving into an apartment for a few months, but soon discarded that idea. There was no sense in going through the agony of moving twice.

We found a house, only to have it fail the inspection. The inspector found signs of a rodent infestation—that fried that prospect for me. The second house—a fifty-year-old one-story in an established neighborhood—looked like the perfect finale to our house-buying history. It needed a bit of work, but it had potential. We fell in love with the bird garden, perfectly manicured lawn, and blooming flowers. The sellers had done the equivalent of Botox and liposuction. Only later did we learn about its structural defects. It needed the equivalent of a heart transplant, colon resection, and major bone repair.

The required inspection uncovered moisture damage under the house. The inspector listed a few other minor problems (one concerning the plumbing). It seemed manageable. We called a contractor to bid on the work and renegotiated the deal. The sellers were eager to close on the house, as they had vacation plans. We set our move-in date, and the structural contractor gave us a timeline. He'd start on a Monday and be finished by the following Friday. Meanwhile no furniture could be placed within six feet of any exterior wall because beams needed replacing.

No problem—we'd fill the garage until the work was completed. We moved the larger furniture indoors, but had the movers stack most of our belongings in the garage. We slept on a pullout sofa in the family room—the only room to have escaped the moisture damage.

We began our quest for a plumber. The first candidate arrived, did a thorough review of the pipes in the crawl-space, and said we needed a complete overhaul. The house had been hooked up to a septic tank at one time and had a strange piping configuration. Pipes that should have led straight to the sewer line doubled back on themselves instead.

He volunteered that he never did this kind of job himself; it was too complicated for him. We called another plumber who failed to show up. We tried a third. This time two men scrambled beneath the house, came back shaking their heads, and said we needed a completely new system. They'd send us a quote, but couldn't begin work for two months. This didn't fit our timetable. We continued to call other plumbers. It was like looking for a vein of silver in a coal mine.

Meanwhile we discovered other problems with the house. It was, after all, a fifty-year-old house with fifty-year-old lighting configurations and kitchen cupboards. The list grew. It didn't make sense to wait to undertake these corrections. We decided on the macro approach. We called a general contractor about updating the house. He couldn't fit us into his calendar for nearly two months.

Things were not going according to plan. The two-week wait for the structural contractor had come and gone, and he was definitely not on schedule. His men had completed the work under the master bedroom, so I enlisted the help of guests to lug our mattress and box spring into the bedroom (Jay was *still* working out of town). It had to be a temporary arrangement, as the bedroom floors needed refinishing. By the time the contractor completed his first month of work on the premises, our timeline matched the plumber's and general contractor's schedules as well.

The seventh week of pounding began beneath the floors when the head carpenter appeared at the front door and announced that he and his assistant would have to stop working. The flooring in the second bathroom had been glued to particleboard and was now coming out in chunks. They needed to replace the beams, and the entire floor and all the fixtures would have to come out before they could continue. He had consulted the company's schedule. They could fit in tearing out the bathroom the following month. I stared at him with an open mouth. I'd been living in this bedlam for seven weeks, and he was consigning me to many, many more.

"If I can get the bathroom torn out by tomorrow, will you continue?"

"Yes."

From three thousand miles away, Jay found a handy-man who made short work of that bathroom. Destruction is *always* easier—just saw that shower in half!

After eight weeks, the work beneath the house was complete. Then the plumbing pandemonium began. The first morning they turned off the water, I needed to use the bathroom. I'm inventive, though. I contemplated lining a five-gallon bucket with a plastic bag and newspapers and heading for the garden shed. I moved to a hotel instead.

By the fourth month, the furniture had been moved from the middle of the living room to the kitchen, family room, out into the garage, to the back patio, and then to the garden shed. What began as an organized move with color-coded boxes had dissolved into chaos. My husband asked me the whereabouts of a certain file. I looked at him in disbelief and threw up my arms.

The general remodel—including rewiring, painting, refinishing the wood floors, and a new kitchen and new bathrooms—required a thousand decisions.

"Ma'am, what color, size, shape, texture—?"

There was no point agonizing over the small things. "It's only a light fixture," became my mantra.

A friend endured an elongated renovation time. She treated every decision as if it were of major significance. My refrain was: "Let's keep this project moving."

As with every renovation, there were unexpected surprises. The new microwave (made by the company whose repairman is never busy) managed to quit every time after one minute of use. A flabbergasted repairman discovered that the factory had installed the fan backwards. After all the changes, the roof sprang a leak and stained a newly painted ceiling. Eventually the day arrived when the project was pronounced complete—just in time for the holidays.

The experience of remodeling is like having a baby in more ways than just the length of the process. The trauma and agony of labor are soon forgotten in the joy of a new child—or in an updated abode.

A Little Exercise in the Garden

O ften when our adult children call, they'll ask, "What's going on there?"

I give an innocuous response. "Oh, the usual—gardening, trips to the gym . . . "

This doesn't cover half of it. As they say—the devil is in the details.

Last week Jay and I spent hours spreading compost, digging, and cultivating the vegetable garden. We mulched the paths and then turned our attention to the small patches of lawn.

Winter weather in the Northwest provides an ideal climate for moss growth in the lawn. Beneath those first, brave blades of grass is a thick, lime-green carpet of suffocating, fuzzy nap. Left to its own devices, it will over-take and kill the grass. One of our yearly gardening chores is ridding the lawn of this plague. The multistep process begins by spraying an organic compound on the lawn, which is designed to kill this matted undergrowth. Once the moss turns an ugly black, it's time for the second step—raking it out. Flimsy plastic rakes that sweep leaves and pine needles in the fall are useless for combing out moss. Only a heavy iron rake will do.

As I chopped and hacked with my tool at the tenacious tentacles, it reminded me of combing a rat's nest of tangles out of a child's cropped curls.

I attacked the patches of moss, tugging and pulling. Soon sweat was rolling down my forehead and into my eyes. It was time for a break. I wiped my forehead with a sleeve, propped my rake, and headed for the shed to get a waste bin—a green, fifty-gallon container made of heavy plastic and mounted on two wheels. A huge hinged cover flops open, its lip resting on the ground while the bin is being filled. Once the container is full, the lid falls forward over the top to seal it.

It's easy enough to move the bin when it's empty. Unfortunately this bin was not empty—it was half-full of moldy grass clippings. I grabbed the imbedded metal handle, tipped the container back to engage the wheels, and staggered toward the nearest piles of desiccated moss. I parked the vessel on the garden path and began filling it. As I worked, I needed to move it a few feet closer to the next piles. The cover was flipped open; no need to close it for this little move. I grabbed the handle to push the bin forward and stepped on the lower edge of the cover as I pushed the container. My foot prevented the cover from moving. The lower part of the bin lurched forward as the top was held fast by my foot. The bin—now tipping on its back—exerted sudden force on the lid, converting it into a slingshot. It launched me headfirst into bin contents of mushy grass and decaying moss.

I screamed. My leg hit the hinge with a thud. For a moment I was dazed; my head was covered in muck. Then, spitting mouthfuls of grass, my feet slipping and sliding on the lid, I scrambled to get out. I slid off the lid and laboriously righted myself. Furtive glances at the fence assured me that no neighbor had witnessed my plight. I began wildly brushing at my hair, face, and clothes to dislodge the globs of slimy crud. I blew grass from my nose. I cursed and massaged my injured leg.

Later I took another break—a safer sort. I found a resting spot on a bench. Jay's eyes narrowed as he surveyed me.

"You've got grass clippings all over the back of your shirt. What happened?"

Visions of me as swamp monster flickered across my mind. "Just a little yoga in the garden."

With the Best of Intentions

Homemade gifts are hyped as being better, more personal, and one of a kind. They're far superior to a traditional Mother's Day gift of a toaster or a Father's Day gift of a tie. The giver of a homemade gift has dedicated hours of time to create something special.

It was with this notion embedded in my psyche that I embarked on a project to knit a ski sweater for Jay's Christmas present. My grandmother and mother had taught me how to cast on stitches and to knit and purl, but beyond that, I had no formal knitting training. How hard could it be to read the directions and follow the instructions on the diagrams?

I bought the required skeins of acrylic yarn in shades of aqua, blue, red, and white. (Jay's allergic to wool.) The brochure illustrated the finished product: a long-sleeved sweater with an elaborate, multicolored pattern across the chest. I envisioned Jay, the colored pattern marching across his chest, swelling with pride. His *loving wife* had created this art. I worked on the project when Jay was out of town—which was easy since he traveled half the time.

Night after night, I knitted feverishly. Soon I had pieces of sleeves and the back of the sweater in knitted rows of aqua yarn. I hadn't begun the front—the most difficult section. The amount of time required to finish the sweater grew exponentially.

In early December, I capitulated and purchased a gift for Jay. The intended Christmas present had morphed into his February birthday present. As Jay's birthday grew closer, I became more harried. The large, flat parts of the sweater were not difficult; it was simply a matter of knitting long rows. However, the sections where the number of stitches had to be increased or decreased demanded closer attention.

This was nothing compared to knitting the striped pattern across the chest: pick up one color, drop another, drag the yarn along the inside of the garment, and count stitches. I found myself holding the yarns tightly in my fist, concentrating. The pattern began to materialize with its little red, blue, and white shapes. I could see the end of the project measured in hours, not days. To my dismay, I found that the emerging product reflected my increased concentration— the stitches had become smaller and tighter. The lovely stripe across the chest seemed shrunken. Perhaps blocking and steaming would resolve the problem, I thought, so I plugged away, racing to the finish line.

I whipped the pieces together and began the process known as blocking. One advantage of acrylic yarn is that it keeps its shape. The advantage was now the disadvantage. The stripe could not be coaxed into stretching itself loosely across the front piece. When I held the sweater up for review, the stripe looked like a girdle binding the chest. Maybe it would stretch out with a few washings.

Jay unfolded the aqua offering from its tissue paper. "Wow, you did this? Aren't you amazing!" He pulled the bulky garment over his head and stretched to free his hands—and kept stretching.

I gazed at him in horror. The arms! What had happened to that measurement? His hands were swathed in aqua knit. The cuffs had to be turned up to his elbows before his hands were visible. Could I loosen the chest stripe *and* shrink the sleeves?

"You are a sweetheart. It's beautiful," he said, wrapping his acrylic-encased arms around me. It *was* one of a kind.

In the evenings, he now sits covered by a long, carefully knitted, cream-colored wrap. I've graduated to knitting afghans.

Wrong Turn, No Turn

Last summer Jay and I took a long driving trip across Washington, Idaho, Montana, and Wyoming, heading for a spot near Denver. We shared the driving, dividing it into two-hour stints with breaks to stretch legs, loosen joints, and keep minds alert. When it was my turn, I settled behind the wheel in mid-Montana to cruise along at seventy-plus miles per hour. There were few vehicles on that long stretch of road.

I am a model driver. I never use a cell phone or let my eyes stray to a computer screen while driving. (I'm quite self-righteous in this stance.) To make the trip more bearable, I listened to an audio book—a mystery with a page-turning plot—or in this case, an ear-engaging plot.

My eyes were fixed on the road—too fixed. I spaced out those huge metal poles supporting highway signs that signaled a turn in our road. Could there be two interstates in this deserted part of the country? Apparently so! The road turning south was an interstate, but so was the one going straight ahead. Two roads diverged on the plain, and I took the one less traveled by; I aimed the car straight ahead.

Ninety minutes later, I read the words "Bismarck, North Dakota" on a mileage sign. I gulped.

"Uhhh…" I sought Jay's opinion. "Should we be on the road to North Dakota?"

He answered with a sigh. I turned off the CD player and began a desperate search for an exit. Jay pulled out the map to look for any road that angled back to the other interstate. If there was a cow path, he couldn't find it. A sign loomed ahead of us: "Next exit, fifty miles."

How dreadful it feels to zoom along a road with every turn of the tires taking you further from your destination. Finally I spotted an emergency vehicle turnoff cutting through the median dividing the interstate. With neither car nor truck visible in any direction, my vehicle became an emergency vehicle. I zipped across and U-turned to retrace our path. Jay was the model of restraint, never again mentioning our four-hour detour.

Perhaps life is like that—sometimes you are distracted by the noise around you and you miss the big signs and guideposts steering you in another direction. What should you do then? Look for cow paths. If you fail to find them, commit some minor lawbreaking—make a U-turn and retrace your steps.

All was not lost. We were safe, together, and the road went on. Memo to self—avoid listening to engrossing mysteries while driving.

Forgive Us Our Trespasses, Overlook Our Mistakes

How does a marriage survive fifty years and counting? Our pastor, in his premarital counseling session all those years ago, knew the answer when he asked, "Do you *like* each other?"

Liking denotes friendship—overlooking the foolish, impulsive, careless, and thoughtless word or deed. After all these years together, we know each other's faults and weaknesses, and we never capitalize on them. A crucial trait of friendship is the lack of criticism. Every one of us has thrown out his line and come up with a dead fish. It's so much better to laugh and go on! I've kept a log of my mistakes—Jay has not.

There is another side to this coin: while ignoring the worst, support and give encouragement to your partner's best traits and instincts. I'm a better person for having entered into this marriage contract all those years ago. Jay has given me time, money, space, and encouragement. Where would I be were it not for him? He was delighted when I went back to school to update my skills so that I could enter a profession after the children were in school.

He has listened to my hopes and dreams and joined whole-heartedly in my projects.

"You want a garden? I can put in a watering system; I'll help you weed the garden. You want to write? I'll read what you've written and give you constructive feedback and praise. You have a basket full of rejection letters? I'll commiserate with you, expounding on the poor taste of the reviewer who missed the great opportunity to publish your works. You want to improve your body and health? I'll go to the gym with you and join you on those long walks."

The answer to our pastor of years gone by is "yes." We *like* each other. Who could ask for more?

ACKNOWLEDGMENTS

"Confessions of an Inept Mechanic" and "I'll Take a Teenager Any Day" appeared in *The Kansas City Times* with different titles and under the pseudonym Robin R. James.

Abbreviated versions of "Cobwebs on the Chandelier," "A Wet Blanket," and "Yard Fight: Woman Versus Squirrel" have been published in *Northwest Prime Time.*

I am deeply indebted to my writer friends, Sallie Glerum and Ginny NiCarthy, for their professional expertise, for their faith and encouragement in bringing this project to completion, and most of all, for their friendship.